Paolo Scotto

WINE AND CHEESE OF ITALY

With the collaboration of the
Istituto Europeo di Design
Rome

GREMESE

To my wife Francesca,
smiling companion of adventures
in art, culture and gastronomy

ACKNOWLEDGEMENTS
The Publisher and the Author wish to thank the trade consortia and wine and cheese producers who supplied many of the illustrations.
Special thanks also go to chef Antonello Colonna, maître fromager Alberto Marcomini of Venice, Emilio Volpetti of the excellent delicatessen on Via Marmorata in Rome, and Fabio Turchetti of "L'Espresso" *guide.*
Special thanks also to Franco Ricci, editor-in-chief of Il Sommelier Italiano *and the Italian Sommelier Association from whose lovely book all the maps of regional wines of Denominated Origin were taken.*

A special thanks to Istituto Europeo di Design in Rome and to Antonio Barrella and Vitaliano Lopez who co-ordinated the photography work of Davide Monteleone, Federica Rosa, Alessandra Manca, Fabio Cuttiga, Elena Cornalis mentioned below.

Original title: Formaggi e Vini d'Italia
© 1997 Gremese Editore S.r.l.

Translated from the Italian by: Laura Clarke

Editor: Laura Clarke

Cover by: Carlo Soldatini

Photographs by: Giorgio De Camillis (p.p. 9, 11, 17, 23, 32, 35, 40, 41, 45, 47, 53, 55, 56, 58, 59, 61, 62, 64, 66, 67, 69); Davide Monteleone (p. 19); Federica Rosa (p. 27); Alessandra Manca (p.p. 29, 31, 33 bottom, 43 top, 65, 70); Fabio Cuttiga (p. 50); Elena Cornalis (p. 60). All the other photographs were kindly supplied by the consortia and producers whom we thank.

Photocomposition and photolithography, Gescom S.r.l. - Viterbo

Printed and bound by: Grafedit S.p.a. - Bergamo

GREMESE
First Edition © 1999
New Books s.r.l.
Via Virginia Agnelli, 88 - 00151 Rome
Tel.: +39/06 65740507 Fax: +39/06 65740509
E-mail: gremese@gremese.com

website: http://www.gremese.com

ISBN 88-7301-301-5

CONTENTS

PREFACE

*I*n Italy the alarm has been sounding for some time already: wine consumption is falling, particularly among young people. Of course, there is comfort in the fact that, although intake is down, quality is on the up. This is due to a network of producers who, through the rejection of rigid policies and constraints of local traditions, have managed to establish new frontiers in the enjoyment of wine. The vineyards and the wine cellars have been overhauled, and the results are promising for the future. The problem, however, is that the prevailing concern with such matters as health and, all too often, a careless marketing campaign, have together led to the loss of precious time in capturing the markets.

Nevertheless, considerable praise must go to the Associazione Italiana dei Sommelier which, through its excellent courses, has over the years created a generation of professionals who have raised the standard of the wine on offer in the cellars of Italy's best restaurants. These courses have also generated a large number of enthusiastic men and women whose only desire has been to learn about the various aspects of the wine culture: regional denominations, principles of tasting, comparative trials, the technique of wine-making, etc.

In this respect, praise must also go to Carlo Petrini's organization Slow Food, which has for a long time been acting in defense of the roots of Italy's alimentary culture. It is as a result of this group's enthusiasm that Cheese, the first European exposition of Italian and European cheeses to be awarded the Protected Guarantee of Origin by the European Union, took place in September 1997. In four days, this large popular festival attracted one hundred thousand visitors to Bra, a small, "old Piedmont" town.

The public is not lacking in enthusiasm or curiosity. What is needed, however, is a lesson in making a discerning choice from among the innumerable products on the market. The transformation of the daily ritual of mealtimes into a pleasure instead of a monotonous appointment is up to us alone. As Paul Bocuse, one of the fathers of modern cooking, used to say, you need to start with the market and the products. And wine is a marvelous "living" product, able to give us intense moments both gastronomic and spiritual.

INTRODUCTION

In Italy "the kingdom of Bacchus" is the subject of a number of serious and highly specialized publications which steer us through the labyrinth of the numerous DOC (Controlled Denomination of Origin), DOGC (Controlled and Guaranteed Denomination of Origin), and (major) table wines by providing tables, evaluations and highly detailed information. These are immensely valuable texts which have had – and continue to have – no small hand in promoting good wine. Our intention, however, is completely different. Taking cheese as our starting point, we have tried simply to generate curiosity by highlighting in as "unesoteric" a way as possible the facts and products of which you need to be aware before you start to experiment, so that you do not get lost among the shelves of Italy's ever more encyclopedic wine cellars.

Emphasis on the pleasure of drinking the "right" glass of wine and on the improvement of a cheese with the "right" bottle (especially when the cheese in question is a minor masterpiece of Italian culinary craftsmanship) seemed therefore to take priority over pedantic research into the mysteries and secrets of Italian wine production.

For this reason, while fully recognizing the arbitrariness of the choice, we have indicated with a heart those wines which, though not necessarily the "best" wines from each region, nevertheless have qualities which make them a good accompaniment to our cheeses. Some will criticize the fact that we have not indicated the vintage, but this was also a deliberate choice. Of course wine is a living product and each vintage has its own history; but to throw an enthusiastic beginner into the often difficult investigation of rare and exquisite vintages seemed to risk burdening him prematurely, when my aim was simply to create an opportunity for a discussion about food. It is for this reason also that, for every region of Italy, I have tried to evoke some aspects of the gastronomic tradition. Wine, food and cheese are not separate realities. On the contrary, in each location they make up a whole which bears witness to its gastronomic roots.

Castelmagno cheese, Barbaresco, Agnolotti: there is no better synthesis of the culinary tradition in Piedmont, for example.

In short, over and above its academic aspects, cooking must first and foremost be about love of experimentation. It is only in this way, through trial and error, that you can develop a taste for food and a love of wine, discovering for yourself just how much culture and civilization can be squeezed into a simple glass of wine or a slice of cheese.

VALLE D'AOSTA

Favorite Wines

**Vallée d'Aoste Blanc
de Morgex et de La Salle -
La Cave du Vin Blanc**
Robiola di Roccaverano

**Vallée d'Aoste Chambave
Moscato Passito -
La Crotta di Vegneron**
Castelmagno

The cuisine in Valle d'Aosta speaks the language of butter. Butter is, in fact, the main ingredient in the highly calorific traditional regional recipes - simple dishes, to be sure, conceived in the shadow of the alpine pastures, but no less tasty for all that. Fondue undoubtedly takes pride of place. It is a creamy masterpiece made from milk, eggs and delicious Fontina, the most famous cheese in the valley and an important ingredient in the preparation of another local specialty, *costolette di vitello alla valdostana,* breaded cutlets of veal fried in butter. Contrary to the Mediterranean tradition with its emphasis on pasta, in Valle d'Aosta first course dishes revolve around polenta and soups, such as the classic *valpellinentze,* made from Savoy cabbage, Fontina and beef stock. Cold cuts also deserve a special mention, including the tasty *mocetta* (like *bresaola* but coming from the haunch of the chamois or goat), the fragrant Arnad bacon and the *boudin,*

The vineyards in Valle d'Aosta are "alpine" in nature.

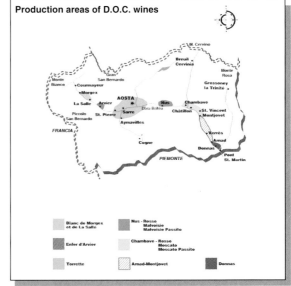

Production areas of D.O.C. wines

Blanc de Morgex et de La Salle

Enfer d'Arvier

Torrette

Nus - Rosso
Malvoisie
Malvoisie Passito

Chambave - Rosso
Moscato
Moscato Passito

Arnad-Montjovet

Donnas

sausages made from pig's blood, potatoes and spices. The accompanying wine tradition is also interesting, even if arguably it has not yet reached its full potential. Viticulture in the valley goes back a long way. Some people date it to the native Salassi population, others to the Romans. Whatever the case, there are documents dating from 1200 which testify to the way in which the clergy used to urge the local peasants to cultivate terrain suitable for growing vines. More recently, the Regional Agricultural Institute has taken a pioneering role in initiatives to improve the quality of the wine in what is, in fact, the smallest wine-producing region in Italy. The vineyards are located on both sides of the Dora Baltea, covering an area of a little over 1000 hectares. In the Bassa Valle, closer to Piedmont, Nebbiolo and red wines such as the pleasant, almond-flavored Donnas prevail. The central area, on the other hand, is home to the austere Chambave Rosso and to Chambave Moscato Passito, whose rich complex bouquet of ripe fruit makes it an ideal accompaniment for austere, mature cheeses such as Castelmagno or Ragusano. Moving up towards the Alta Valle, there is Enfer d'Arvier, which is similar to the Savoyard Mondeuse, vigorous, with a harmonious taste of pine. Blanc de Morgex et de La Salle is a unique wine which is produced from one of the few vine plants in the world to grow on steep slopes well above 1000 meters. Delicate and with a slight aftertaste of herbs, this white can rightly be considered alpine. It goes well with a mild Robiola.

♥ *Vallée d'Aoste Chambave Moscato Passito - Ezio Voyat*
Made from white muscat grapes, this high-altitude Passito is the only one of its kind. Notable for its intense golden color and density, it has an aromatic bouquet and a strong, pleasant, fruity taste. It contrasts nicely with a Fiore Sardo cheese.

PIEDMONT

April 29 1859: the region of Piedmont had just declared war on Austria, and the Prime Minister, Camille Cavour, could proclaim with satisfaction: "Today we have made history. Now let's go and eat." The story is a good one because it sums up the spirit of Piedmont: solidity, moderation, a slight formalism, but also a sincere love of good food. Here, however, the cuisine has never succumbed to the exponents of creative extravagance, or to the Mediterranean obsession with extra-virgin olive oil. In Piedmont, in fact, the spaghetti

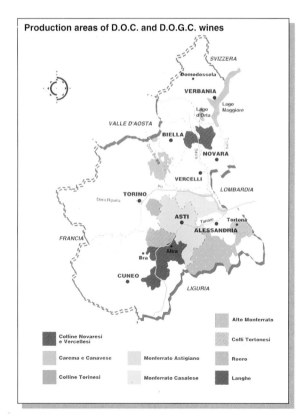

Production areas of D.O.C. and D.O.G.C. wines

Muscat grapes being harvested.

culture holds little sway (except in Alba with its classic *tajarin all'uovo*), while enthusiasm for food and the ingredients for the risotto which is so dear to the Piedmontese both have their home in the wide plains between Vercelli and Novara. This is all that the region has to offer as far as first course dishes are concerned (the exceptions are *agnolotti*, which are best eaten in soup form (they are improved still further if a dash of Barbera is added) and *col plin*, the Asti pasta dish served with butter). All dishes can, however, be readily combined with another totem of the regional cuisine: the unsurpassable and highly expensive white *tartufo*.

These diverse flavors unite to form an ancient and solid gastronomic tradition, in which the male world of hunters and vine-dressers is juxtaposed against the female world of the capable housewives who guard the secrets of flan pastry, ragout, sweets, and baked

custard. In short, Piedmont is indisputably a region in which the Italian gastronomic tradition is at its height, presenting a palette of surprising contrasts, from the strong aroma of the oil in *bagna cauda* (an oil-based sauce with abundant garlic and anchovies) served with the delicious cardoon from Monferrato and a host of other vegetables, to the delicacy of the chocolate and dessert-making traditions.

This being the case, it would have been a cruel trick of fate had the region been able to boast only a modest wine tradition. Instead, thanks in particular to its exceptional red wines, Piedmont has a good reputation throughout the world and produces a number of

Favorite Wines

Barbaresco Sorì San Lorenzo - A. Gaja
Parmigiano Reggiano

Barbaresco Riserva Paje - Produttori del Barbaresco
Fiore Sardo

Barolo Vigna Colonnello - A. Conterno
Grana Padano

Barolo Cannubi - P. Scavino
Bitto

Dolcetto d'Alba Coste & Fossati - G.D. Vajra
Toma

Vigna Larigi (barbera) - E. Altare
Casciotta di Urbino

Gavi di Gavi Etichetta Nera - La Scolca
Taleggio

Novara hills and Vercelli
Production areas of D.O.C. and D.O.C.G. wines

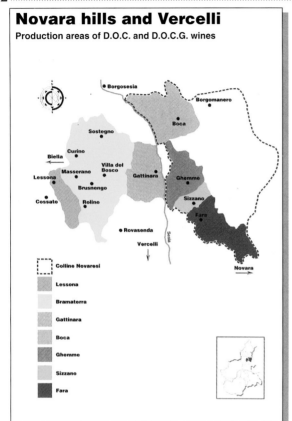

Colline Novaresi

- Lessona
- Bramaterra
- Gattinara
- Boca
- Ghemme
- Sizzano
- Fara

Monferrato
Production areas on D.O.C. and D.O.C.G. wines

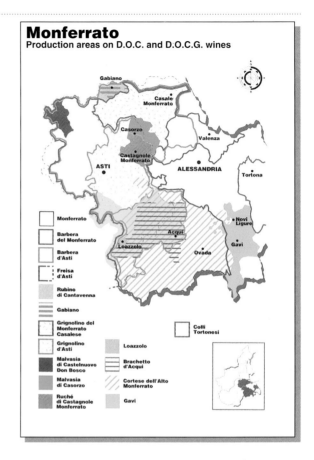

- Monferrato
- Barbera del Monferrato
- Barbera d'Asti
- Freisa d'Asti
- Rubino di Cantavenna
- Gabiano
- Grignolino del Monferrato Casalese
- Grignolino d'Asti
- Malvasia di Castelnuovo Don Bosco
- Malvasia di Casorzo
- Ruché di Castagnole Monferrato
- Loazzolo
- Brachetto d'Acqui
- Cortese dell'Alto Monferrato
- Gavi
- Colli Tortonesi

Barbaresco can be considered one of the 19th century forerunners to the great "noble" wines.

Langhe and Roero
Production areas of D.O.C. and D.O.C.G. wines

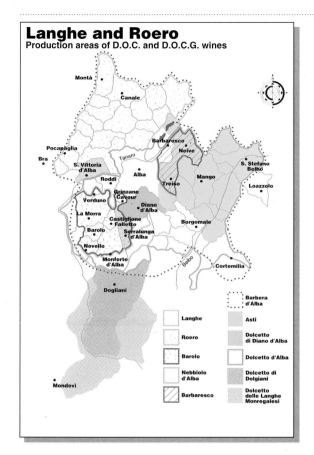

Piedmont
Production areas of Dolcetti D.O.C. wines

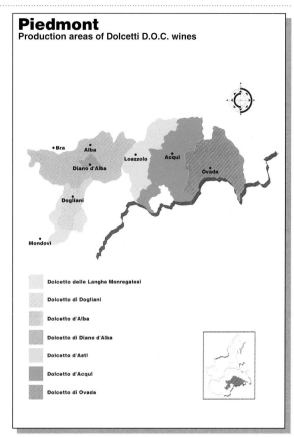

"characteristic" wines whose quality is improving, due in part to a policy of modernization adopted by the majority of cellars and pioneered by Angelo Gaja, producer of the best wines in the region. Barolo and Barbaresco are the two principal gems and take their name from two fortified settlements in the hills. They are both made from *nebbiolo* grapes and can be considered the 19th century forerunners to all the "noble" wines that were to follow. Complex and austere, they are notable for their high tannin content and for their ability to withstand aging, qualities which make them perfect to accompany "regal" cheeses such as Parmigiano Reggiano or a

A bunch of muscat grapes which produce a unique dessert wine.

Nebbiolo grapes are used to make the finest wines in Piedmont: Barolo, Barbaresco and Gattinara.

mature Asiago, rather than a classic Castelmagno. The family of wines produced from the *nebbiolo* grape is in fact very large: the robust Carema is produced on the borders of the Valle d'Aosta, while Bramaterra, Lessona, Boca, Ghemme and the famous Gattinara are produced in the areas around Novara and Vercelli. In spite of their differences, these reds are all rich in flavor and have impact, making them ideal companions to the classic local cheeses: Bra, Raschera or Murazzano, for example.

The river Tanaro separates the Langa and the Roero wine regions, which are home to Dolcetto, Barbera, Freisa and also Arneis (produced exclusively in the Roero). The latter is a white wine with a pleasant, fruity bouquet and a dry, pure taste which make it suitable to accompany a delicate Robiola.

This cheese can also be accompanied by the crisp and refreshing Gavi, another classic white from the hills in southern

The Barbaresco vineyards benefit from the sharp contrast between summer and winter temperatures.

The Scarpa cellars at Nizza Monferrato, in the heart of a region which produces an excellent Barbera.

Alessandria, near the border with Liguria.
The Asti area must be considered separately. This is home to Barbera, a pure, striking wine which goes well with a Quartirolo or a medium-ripe Pecorino Sardo. In addition to pleasant and easily drinkable reds such as Grignolino, however, this area also owes its reputation to *muscat*, a vine unrivaled in the production of sweet wines, many of which are then sparkled, or turned into Moscato d'Asti, a clean, fragrant dessert wine with a strong bouquet and a very low alcohol content (about 5.5%).

♥ **Barbaresco Sorì Tildìn - A. Gaja**
This fine red made from nebbiolo grapes is the result of a dream inspired by French examples (Piedmont-born Angelo Gaja has appropriated the idea of the harvest or "cru" and the intelligent use of storage barrels). It stands apart from its twin, Sorì San Lorenzo, another quality Barbaresco produced by the Gaja estate, because of the location of the wine production area (colder and higher) and its full-bodied elegance. Its balanced taste of violets and berries make it an ideal accompaniment to Castelmagno.

LIGURIA

Drawing strength from an exceptionally good extra-virgin olive oil, the cuisine in Liguria has clear Mediterranean overtones. Its recipes are rooted in the immutable customs of the taciturn seamen and the agriculturists who have been cultivating their products on the narrow strip of land between the mountains and the sea from time immemorial. Here bread is substituted by *focaccia*, which is eaten universally. It is a versatile food, and is delicious in a classic combination with cheese, or in a more daring combination with onion. Basil follows close behind, and in Liguria it boasts a unique smell and a salty taste which is the basis for one of the internationally renowned Italian sauces, *pesto*, made from basil garlic, pine kernels and grated Pecorino.

On the other hand, tomatoes, onions, olives, eggs, and tuna roe combine with *galletta* to make *condiggion*, a delicious seafood dish which can be prepared in a number of different ways. The dessert-making tradition is also well developed (the port at Genoa became the landing stage for hundreds of spices in the

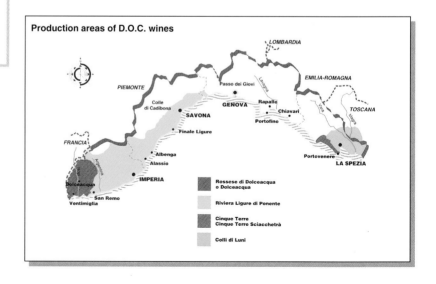

Production areas of D.O.C. wines

The Cascina Terre Rosse cellars at Finale Ligure: technology and tradition exist side by side.

Middle Ages), and includes biscuits, such as *canestrelli*, *amaretti* from Sasselo, *Baci* from Alassio, and the delicious *pandolce*, a modest alternative to the more "worldly" *panettone*. The regional wine industry is still fragmented and consists of a scattering of small businesses;

In Cinque Terre the grape harvest was once gathered onto boats.

but, although it has not yet managed to fulfill its qualitative potential, production is on the up. The province of La Spezia, near the Tuscan border, is home to Vermentino di Luni, a pure and interesting wine thought to have descended from the product described by Pliny in ancient Roman times as the best in Italy: "Etruriae Luna palmam habet". Cinqueterre is practically drawn from the sea (not so long ago, the grape harvest used to be loaded onto small boats), and contains a hint of salt and broom, providing a perfect accompaniment to Taleggio, for example. In contrast, Sciachetrà, another classic wine from this corner of Liguria, goes best with a mature Fiore Sardo or a strong Gorgonzola. Between 18 and 20 kg of grapes are needed to make a single bottle of this palatable but dry wine with a rich bouquet and great allure; the result is truly unique. The area between the far west of the region and Genoa produces two more interesting whites, Vermentino and the more aromatic Pigato, and two pleasant reds, Rossese di Dolceacqua and Ormeasco. Pigato has a full bouquet and a resinous taste which make it an ideal accompaniment to Casciotta di Urbino, while the gentle and fragrant Ormeasco nicely complements a good young Montasio.

♥ *Cinqueterre Sciachetrà -*
Agricultural cooperative of
Riomaggiore, Manarola,
Corniglia, Vernazza and
Monterosso
Between 18 and 20 kg of grapes are needed to make a single bottle of this little known wine. Once harvested, the grapes are placed in a vat, crushed and the juice is boiled for a long time before being drawn off. It is then decanted repeatedly into small casks. The result is a golden medium dry with a rich, balanced bouquet, which goes well with Gorgonzola.

LOMBARDY

The cuisine in Lombardy is muli-faceted - just like the terrain which stretches from the plain to the alpine range. There are some gastronomic constants, of course, such as the prevalence of rice and butter rather than pasta and extra-virgin olive oil, but the generalizations stop here. In mentioning risotto, it is important to remember that this area is home to some of the great national classics, from *risotto alla milanese* (of medieval origin) made using saffron which gives it its yellow color, to the risotto conceived by the monks at the Carthusian monastery in Pavia (from which

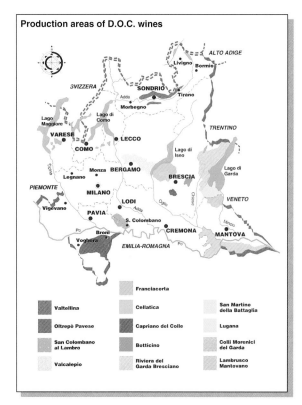

Production areas of D.O.C. wines

Franciacorta

Valtellina

Oltrepò Pavese

San Colombano al Lambro

Valcalepio

Cellatica

Capriano del Colle

Botticino

Riviera del Garda Bresciano

San Martino della Battaglia

Lugana

Colli Morenici del Garda

Lambrusco Mantovano

During the Renaissance, the fine wines served to the Milanese nobility all came from the gentle hills of the Oltrepò, near Pavia.

it takes the name *alla certosina*), in which vegetables are combined with shrimps and frog meat in a subtle blend of flavors. Moving up into the mountains of the Valtellina area, lavish use is made of buckwheat in dishes such as the famous polenta from Tirano, and *pizzoccheri*, thick pasta ribbons served in butter with cheese and Savoy cabbage. Decisive flavors are a characteristic of Lombard cuisine: think no further than the typical *cassoeula* of Milan, a winter dish made from strips of pork and crispy Savoy cabbage. Other dishes with a similar disregard for calorie content are *busecca* (tripe soup typically eaten in Milan), bone marrow (taken from knuckle of veal), and *cotechino*, conceived in Cremona in feudal times as a clever means of using parts of the pig not served to the master. Many dishes have their roots in courtly cuisine, such as the famous Mantuan *tortelli di zucca*, which, like the classic *mostarda* from Cremona, or *casonsei* (whether they come from Bergamo or Brescia is disputable), a sort of *ravioli* stuffed with spinach, raisins and *amaretti*, are a throwback to the tradition of combining sweet and savory tastes. The numerous lakes provide the basic ingredients for an extensive range of fish dishes: carp, tench,

pike, chub and shad (in the Lake Como area, these fish, known as *missoltit*, are sun-dried in the open air and eaten either as an *antipasto* with salt and vinegar or as an accompaniment to polenta) and provide a delicious alternative to the more substantial meat dishes which are so important here. As for desserts (and while still on the subject of gastronomic cornerstones), the fact that the region is home to *panettone*, the totem of Italian Christmas festivities, speaks for itself. In the Lombard region wine-making has also reached remarkable heights. Three wine regions stand out from the rest: Valtellina, Franciacorta and Oltrepò. In Valtellina the

A stage during the production of sparkling wine in famous cellars in Franciacorta.

Province of Brescia
Production areas of D.O.C. wines

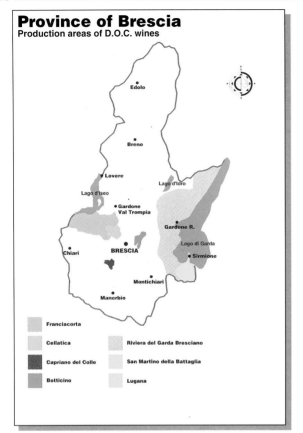

Franciacorta

Cellatica

Capriano del Colle

Botticino

Riviera del Garda Bresciano

San Martino della Battaglia

Lugana

Valtellina
Production areas of D.O.C. wines

Valtellina

Valtellina Superiore
Sassella

Valtellina Superiore
Grumello

Valtellina Superiore
Inferno

Valtellina Superiore
Valgella

terraced vines cling to the rocks up to an altitude of 1000 meters. The most commonly grown vine is *nebbiolo* (called "chiavennasca"), used in the production of prestigious DOC wines such as Grumello, Sassella, Inferno and Sfursat (so called because the harvest and vinification are both delayed). The intense red wines from the Valtellina area, with their strong bouquet and excellent capacity for aging, are a perfect accompaniment to local cheeses such as Bitto and Casera. Thanks to the enthusiasm and courage of a group of clever producers, Franciacorta, situated between Lago d'Iseo and the hills to the north-east of Brescia, has in the last few years become home to some of the finest Italian Champenois, making good use

of the versatile *chardonnay* vine. The hills in the Oltrepò area around Pavia produce more vine than almost any other area in the region. The vines are predominately *barbera*, *croatina*, *pinot nero*, *riesling italico* and *riesling renano*, from which several interesting wines are produced, such as Bonarda, Buttafuoco and numerous sparkling wines.

Lugana, produced on the Brescian side of Lake Garda, also deserves a mention. Made from *trebbiano* grapes, it is an extremely fresh white wine with a delicate fragrance which goes well with Stracchino.

From top to bottom:
Croatina grapes make lively, characterful wines.
Riesling italico produces a sparkling wine which complements the classic fondue from Valle d'Aosta.
Pinot nero is among some of the finest "crus" in Burgundy and is used to make splendid cheese wines.

♥ *Franciacorta Gran Cuvée Pas Operé (dated) - Bellavista*
This exceptionally elegant wine comes from one of the great DOGC sparkling wine regions and is a rival to the finest champagne. Made from a blend of small chardonnay grapes (65%) and pinot nero grapes (35%), it has a lovely, complex aroma and a rich taste which make it ideal to accompany Mozzarella di Bufala Campana.

VENETO

Venetian cuisine has a strong influence on the typical flavors of a region whose climate and landscape vary from the coastal strip to the agricultural plains and the mountains. It goes without saying that fish is predominant; and the flavorsome recipes result from a combination of local tradition and that of the colorful markets of the East, in a lavish counterpoint between rich and poor. The seafood *antipasti* are an absolute must, and include *peoci* (mussels), *cappesante, cappelunghe, garusoli* (murices), clams, *canoce* (mantis prawns), and delicious *granseole* (boiled crabs served in their shell with oil

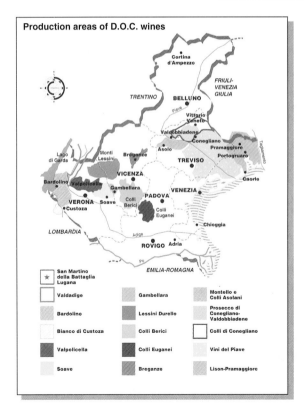

Production areas of D.O.C. wines

★	San Martino della Battaglia Lugana
	Valdadige
	Bardolino
	Bianco di Custoza
	Valpolicella
	Soave
	Gambellara
	Lessini Durello
	Colli Berici
	Colli Euganei
	Breganze
	Montello e Colli Asolani
	Prosecco di Conegliano-Valdobbiadene
	Colli di Conegliano
	Vini del Piave
	Lison-Pramaggiore

The Gavioli vineyards in the heart of the Prosecco wine region.

CANTINA PRODUTTORI DI VALDOBBIADENE

and lemon). Two other protagonists of lagoon cuisine are cuttlefish, whose ink is also used to make the famous *risotto al nero* (do not forget that, in the Verona area, high-quality rice is produced), and *baccalà* (in reality, the Venetians use this name to describe what elsewhere in Italy is called *stoccafisso*), of which the Venetian version made with polenta is famous.

If you prefer meat, there is an infinite choice, from the classic Paduan chicken, to liver with onions *alla veneziana*, and pigeon (the basis for the traditional *sopa coada*, a rich soup from Treviso made from meat stock). The vegetables need a chapter to themselves: the islands in the lagoon are home to delicious and richly-flavored kinds, including artichokes and the famous *castraure* (the small spring vegetable which is delicious when fried), or the red chicory found in Treviso. On the dessert front, in addition to the famous Veronese *pandoro*, the area offers a rich selection of biscuits, including the famous *baicoli* so loved by Goldoni. The wine industry in Veneto is currently undergoing a singular period. After years of intensive production, aimed mainly at the international market, a general

A bunch of prosecco grapes, used to produce some of Italy's best "fizz".

Favorite Wines

Soave Classico Superiore Vigne Vecchie - Gini
Monte Veronese

Amarone - Quintarelli
Asiago

Prosecco di Valdobbiadene-Spumante Dry Garnei - D. Bisol & Figli
Grana Padano

Upper Treviso
Production areas of D.O.C. wines

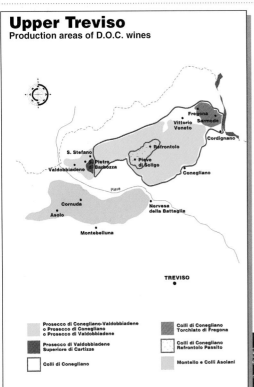

Fregona
Sarmede
Vittorio Veneto
Cordignano
Refrontolo
S. Stefano
Pietro di Barbozza
Valdobbiadene
Pieve di Soligo
Conegliano
Piave
Nervesa della Battaglia
Cornuda
Asolo
Montebelluna
TREVISO

Prosecco di Conegliano-Valdobbiadene
o Prosecco di Conegliano
o Prosecco di Valdobbiadene

Prosecco di Valdobbiadene
Superiore di Cartizze

Colli di Conegliano

Colli di Conegliano
Torchiato di Fregona

Colli di Conegliano
Refrontolo Passito

Montello e Colli Asolani

Provinces of Verona and Gambellara
Production areas of D.O.C. wines

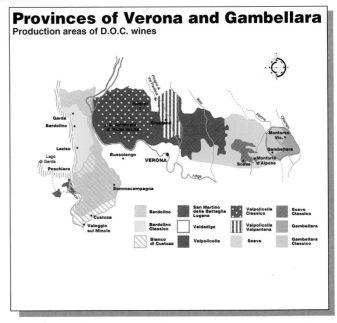

Garda
Bardolino
Lazise
Lago di Garda
Peschiera
Sommacampagna
Custoza
Valeggio sul Mincio
Bussolengo
VERONA
Adige
Montorio Vic.
Gambellara
Monforte d'Alpone
Soave

Bardolino
Bardolino Classico
Bianco di Custoza
San Martino della Battaglia Lugana
Valdadige
Valpolicella
Valpolicella Classico
Valpolicella Valpantena
Soave
Soave Classico
Gambellara
Gambellara Classico

*A typical vineyard
in the Veneto
countryside.*

re-evaluation of quality wine is taking place, as can be seen in Valpolicella and the Prosecco-producing regions between Valdobbiadene and Conegliano. Soave is a classic white wine made from *garganega* and *trebbiano* grapes, which goes well with cheeses such as Taleggio or Mozzarella. It comes from the province of Verona and is probably the most widely-known Veneto wine outside Italy. The hills in the Verona area are home to another internationally renowned wine: the red Valpolicella that ages well. The same grapes are also used to produce Amarone, a warm, intense, full-bodied wine which makes an ideal accompaniment to strong cheeses such as Castelmagno, Parmigiano Reggiano and mature Asiago.

Prosecco, the symbol of the Treviso area, is popular with buyers: it is a gentle, sparkling wine which is drinkable throughout the meal and is characteristically fresh and fragrant.

A lovely bunch of molinara grapes.

♥ Amarone della Valpolicella - Quintarelli
This is a powerful red which, in some vintages, can age for up to ten years in casks. It is a perfect blend of strength, vigor, alcohol, and body with an aroma of spiced fruit resulting from the pressing and aging processes. It goes well with a mature Asiago.

TRENTINO ALTO ADIGE

I n this region two culinary traditions coexist. These have many things in common, but they are also marked by significant differences. The cuisine in Alto Adige is strongly influenced by Austria and Central Europe, while in

Trentino the gastronomy reflects the Veneto tradition. Common to both traditions are *canederli* (known as *knodeln* in the province of Bolzano), a kind of dumpling made from stale bread and a variety of other ingredients which differ from place to place,

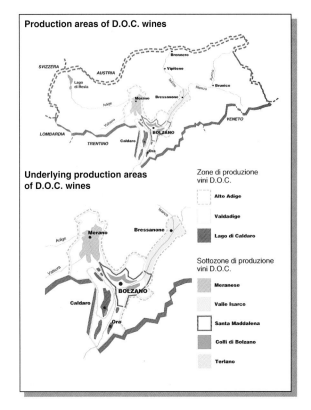

Production areas of D.O.C. wines

Underlying production areas of D.O.C. wines

Zone di produzione vini D.O.C.

- Alto Adige
- Valdadige
- Lago di Caldaro

Sottozone di produzione vini D.O.C.

- Meranese
- Valle Isarco
- Santa Maddalena
- Colli di Bolzano
- Terlano

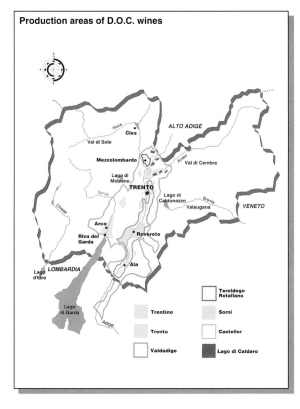

Production areas of D.O.C. wines

- Teroldego Rotaliano
- Trentino
- Sorni
- Trento
- Casteller
- Valdadige
- Lago di Caldaro

The charming Hofstätter di Termeno vineyards (Bolzano).

and can include cheese, smoked ham and chicken liver. Barley soup is also eaten throughout the region and is made from a flavorsome blend of vegetables. Second course dishes in Trentino include *smacafam*, a substantial recipe consisting of oven-baked polenta garnished with bacon and sausage. The numerous game dishes (chamois, roe buck) are of direct Central European descent and are frequently offset by sauces which are bitter or made from fruit such as apples or bilberries.

Goulash is another universal dish (here it appears in an elaborate form), while mushroom-based recipes are equally popular both

The mark of quality of the Trento wines.

Only the finest bunches are harvested in Alto Adige.

TIEFENBRUNNER

Feldmarschall
von Fenner zu Fennberg

in Trentino and Alto Adige. The desserts are inspired by the Austrian tradition, using marzipan, apples and poppy seeds in a number of specialties. As for wine, Trentino and Alto Adige are both major national producers. These regions have managed to produce fine wines of considerable freshness and charm, without failing, however, to keep pace with the renewal of the industry nationally. Recently, a number of very fine wines with surprising structure and complexity have emerged. In Trentino DOC wines have always been given pride of place, to the extent that the entire agricultural area is now devoted exclusively to the cultivation of DOC vines. This is concrete evidence of the existence of a rigorous policy to uphold qualitative standards, the application of which is also guaranteed by the presence of active cooperative cellars. With the exception of Nosiola, a light, fragrant white, Trentino is almost

exclusively a red-producing area. Marzemino, a favorite of Don Giovanni di Mozart, and Teroldego dei Campi Rotaliani, are the two major wines. Both are strongly aromatic and elegant, making a good accompaniment to cheeses of certain texture. Due to the increasing use of the noble and versatile *chardonnay* grape, Trentino has also become one of the national capitals of the sparkling wine industry. The experience of wines from

Alto Adige must begin among the spectacular vineyards of Sankta Magdalener, an area which produces a very interesting red wine, or with the extremely fine red from Lago di Caldaro.

The richly aromatic and suggestive Lagrein is another quality local wine, while Pinot Nero (here known as Blauburgunder), produced by some cellars according to modern criteria, is becoming increasingly popular.

However, mention must also go to the fruity white wines which are produced in the Isarco valley. These elegant wines include Gewürztraminer (made from an ancient, spicy variety of grape), and Muller Thurgau (made from a blend of *riesling* and *sylvaner* grapes which was perfected in Germany towards the end of the 19th century). They both make a pleasing accompaniment to Robiola or a good Mozzarella di Bufala Campana.

♥ *Teroldego Rotaliano Vigneto Sgarzon - Foradori*
Teroldego is striking because of its lovely ruby color and its aroma of fruit and herbs. It is balanced and full-bodied, and instantly pleasing to the palate. Too often undermined by the commercial logic applied by other producers, this real gem is made by one of the most dedicated cellars in the North East. It goes well with Fontina from Valle d'Aosta.

FRIULI VENEZIA-GIULIA

The cuisine in Friuli is associated with images of a family gathering around the fire in front of a large pot of steaming polenta. In reality, however, the regional culinary tradition is extremely varied, reflecting the cultural diversity of an area which has borne the influences of the Venetian and Habsburg empires and the Slavic world at various moments in history. Along the coast for example, the Venetian Empire

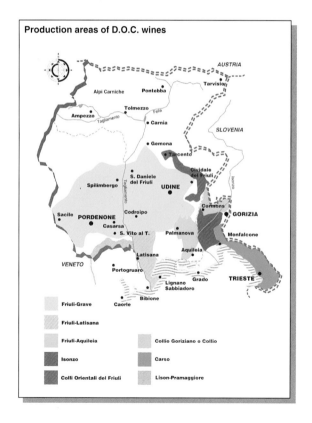

Production areas of D.O.C. wines

Friuli-Grave

Friuli-Latisana

Friuli-Aquileia

Isonzo

Colli Orientali del Friuli

Collio Goriziano o Collio

Carso

Lison-Pramaggiore

CABERNET
Jermann

RONCHI DI CIALLA
COLLI ORIENTALI DEL FRIULI
Denominazione di origine controllata
SCHIOPPETTINO DI CIALLA
Imbottigliato all'origine nei Ronchi di Cialla
nella vendemmia 1993 si sono ottenute
9.202 bottiglie bordolesi, 240 magnum e 24 doppie magnum
0.750l. ℮   Questa bottiglia porta il n. 0000   12,5% vol.

Azienda Agricola Ronchi di Cialla · Prepotto · Italia

has played an important role in determining the numerous local recipes. You need do no more than compare the different kinds of fish soup, from Grado (very garlicky and made from conger eel), to Marano, sieved to obtain a smooth texture, to the soup from Trieste (enhanced with small crustaceans and tomato), in order to realize just how much history and culture can be summed up in a "simple" dish. Inland, the cuisine is dominated by strong, decisive flavors, as in *jota*, a thick soup made from haricot beans, sauerkraut and pork, and the regional version of *cotechino*, served with pickled turnips sautéed in garlic and lard. The complex game dishes echo of central European cuisine, as do

the desserts: *gubana* and *presnitz* (these are identical except for the pastry) made from a skillful blend of hazelnuts, almonds, dried fruit and chocolate.

Two culinary specialties must also get a mention: the sweet San Daniele ham and the rare smoked Sauris ham. Eaten with local cheese, these regional gems make a delicious meal in themselves – all the more so if enjoyed with a good glass of wine.

Thanks to its cool and breezy climate and marly terrain, Friuli produces some of the most singular white wines in Italy. The tradition dates back to ancient times (in a practice which was revolutionary for the period, wine was exported north from the port of Aquileia

Many of the finest wines in Friuli are produced on stony, apparently unproductive terrain.

The idyllic climate in the small area of the East Friuli Hills permits the cultivation of a rich variety of grapes.

in wooden casks rather than traditional amphorae) and enabled the producers to get ahead of their generation, producing elegant, fresh and fruity modern wines, while elsewhere coarse, alcoholic and jaded whites continued to emerge. Today, this tendency – the reason for the success of Friulian wines – has been further developed by the introduction of a series of high-quality labels. The region is also experiencing the effects of a second trend, this time involving the development of more complex whites by experimenting with the grape varieties used to produce the finest wines of the new generation in regions as diverse as Burgundy and California. Separate mention goes to an old and unusual wine, the famous Picolit, which is characterized among other things by extremely limited production. A truly rare wine, it has a distinct aroma and a pleasant, delicate taste which are unmistakable. It is a good accompaniment to Gorgonzola or to mature, flavorsome cheeses.

Friuli produces predominantly white wines, the major ones being Tocai, Ribolla, Sauvignon, Chardonnay and Verduzzo Friulano, produced in the East Friuli Hills (in the province of Udine), Collio Goriziano (the region produces the finest labels), and Grave.

♥ *Chardonnay - Josko Gravner*
Produced by Josko Gravner, this complex Chardonnay is the fruit of enthusiastic and meticulous work in both the vineyards and the cellars. It is undoubtedly an extremely interesting white, and unusual by Italian standards. It is a long-lasting wine with a full body and a complex aroma, and makes a good accompaniment to a classic Toma from Piedmont.

EMILIA ROMAGNA

In the present climate of enthusiasm for the "Mediterranean diet", Emilia Romagna, with its "fatty" buttery dishes, has lost some of its status as the gastronomic capital of traditional Italian cuisine – a status strongly linked to the work of Artusi but also rooted in historical evidence: Bologna University library houses the manuscript of the *Libro de arte coquinaria,* the first known text relating to the history of culinary art in Italy, drawn up by Maestro Martino in the mid-15th century.

In fact Emilia and Romagna have very different histories, flavors and traditions. Common to both cuisines, however, is home-made pasta, bearing witness to the skill of the local women and the starting point for infinite variations: *tortelli, tagliatelle* (a culinary cornerstone), *lasagne,* and various kinds of stuffed pasta, including *garganelli,*

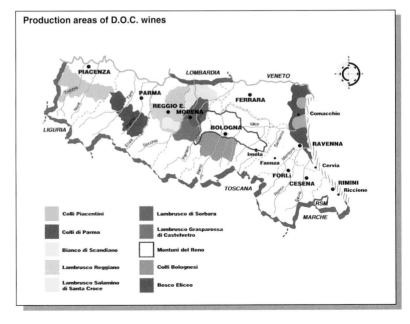

Production areas of D.O.C. wines

Colli Piacentini	Lambrusco di Sorbara
Colli di Parma	Lambrusco Grasparossa di Castelvetro
Bianco di Scandiano	Montuni del Reno
Lambrusco Reggiano	Colli Bolognesi
Lambrusco Salamino di Santa Croce	Bosco Eliceo

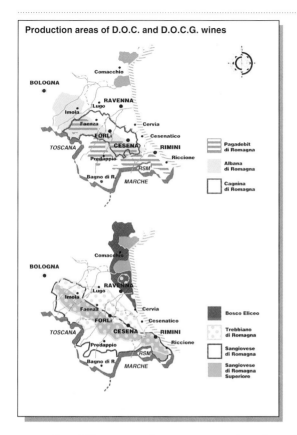

Production areas of D.O.C. and D.O.C.G. wines

BOLOGNA
Comacchio
RAVENNA
Imola
Lugo
Faenza
Cervia
FORLÌ
Cesenatico
TOSCANA
CESENA
RIMINI
Predappio
Riccione
RSM
Bagno di R.
MARCHE

Pagadebit di Romagna
Albana di Romagna
Cagnina di Romagna

BOLOGNA
Comacchio
RAVENNA
Imola
Lugo
Faenza
Cervia
FORLÌ
Cesenatico
TOSCANA
CESENA
RIMINI
Predappio
Riccione
RSM
Bagno di R.
MARCHE

Bosco Eliceo
Trebbiano di Romagna
Sangiovese di Romagna
Sangiovese di Romagna Superiore

A 15th-century fortress houses the Romagna Regional Wine Cellar in Dozza, near Imola.

cappellacci (the type using pumpkin from Ferrara is excellent), *anolini* (typical of Parma and Reggio Emilia), and the mythical *tortellini* from Bologna.

Notable among second course dishes are *bollito misto*, rivalled only in Piedmont, and the mushrooms from the Taro Valley, which are thought to be the finest in Italy. However, pork is the basic ingredient in a series of products which best characterize the regional cuisine, from Parma and Langhirano ham to *culatello*, Felino salami to *coppe*, *cotechini* and *zamponi*. Mention must also be made of the unique and higly expensive traditional balsamic vinegar which is produced in Modena and Reggio Emilia. It dates back to the time of Matilde of Canossa, who thought it

flavorsome fish soup and fried fish. *Passatelli* (a kind of short spaghetti made from breadcrumbs, egg and parmesan cheese) in broth also comes from here. It is now an "international" dish thanks to its popularity with tourists who visit the Romagna coast.

The regional wines are not unlike the local inhabitants in character: strong, pleasant and direct – qualities which have earned their products the reputation of being "popular wines". The period of intensive production and exportation of poor quality wines to the United States having come to an end, the vines are currently undergoing a deliberate overhaul. Lambrusco (or Sorbara, Grasparossa di Castelvetro or Salamino as it is

sufficiently valuable to give to the visiting emperor as a gift. Balsamic vinegar is obtained from refined must, and its unmistakable flavor lends character to a number of dishes, from a simple steak to a fruit salad of strawberries.

Romagna is home to a number of fish dishes, including

Sangiovese vineyards deep within attractive countryside with a wealth of history.

variously called) remains a classic wine from Emilia. It is a fragrant red, fresh and pleasant on the palate. Gutturnio is an excellent red which comes from the hills around Piacenza. Its bouquet and taste are reminiscent of the classic reds from the Oltrepò, near Pavia. Romagna is dominated by Sangiovese, a full-bodied, fragrant wine which is an ideal accompaniment to mild cheeses such as Pecorino Toscano or a mild Bra. However, the real masterpiece is Albana which, in its white variety, has an aroma of vanilla and honey and a taste that is unbelievably warm and soft. Comparable to the prestigious French Sauternes, it is a perfect complement to Gorgonzola or a mature Fiore Sardo.

Proof of its excellence is found in the legend claiming that when the Empress Galla Placidia took a sip of this wine presented to her in a humble cup by a peasant farmer, she exclaimed: "Vorrei berti in oro" ("I want to drink it from gold"). This phrase is the origin of the name of the town of Bertinoro in the heart of the Albana region.

♥ *Lambrusco Vigna Ca' del Fiore - Manicardi*
This lively red is frequently dismissed as being an unpretentious, low-quality sparkling wine for undemanding consumers. However, its taste reveals a pleasant combination of freshness, fragrance and balance. In short, it is a good match for a classic Quartirolo from Lombardy.

TUSCANY

Tuscany represents a kind of cultural hinge between the South, with its Mediterranean tradition and its pasta, and the North with its rice, butter and polenta. It extends from rugged Maremma to the gentle Chianti hills, a vast area reflected in the number of culinary traditions which converge here. Common to all traditions, however, is the fruity aroma of the extra-virgin olive oil which is used in almost every recipe, from simple toasted bread rubbed with garlic to *fettunta*, or the delicious soups which are the real mainstay of the Tuscan diet: think no further than the pasta served with beans (better still if made with *cannellini* from Sorano), *ribollita*, a spectacular blend of beans, bread and red cabbage, or the famous *pappa al pomodoro*, also made from bread with tomatoes, leeks, basil and a hint of ginger. Pasta enthusiasts must try the Sienese *pici*, or *pinci*, large spaghetti made from flour and water and served in a garlicky sauce.

Slow aging in barrels gives Antinori wines the special characteristics which guarantee their quality in the line-up of great Tuscan wines.

An authentic Tuscan meal should begin with flavorsome *crostini* (thick slices of toasted bread) with chicken livers, followed by soup and then meat: the classic *fiorentina* (a thick rib steak), stewed wild boar (the symbolic dish of the cowmen and hunters in the Maremma area), or delicious tripe, the traditional staple of the Florentine poor. Rivalling these meat dishes in flavor is *cacciucco*, the classic seafood dish from Livorno made from lean fish, garlic and chili, which begs to be accompanied by a red wine. Tuscan biscuits are renowned for their excellence (these include *cantuccini* and *ghiottini*), as is the more complex *panforte* from Siena, a dessert which has echoes of its medieval origins.

As for wines, today Tuscany ranks among one of the top red-producing regions. Praise must go to the producers who have

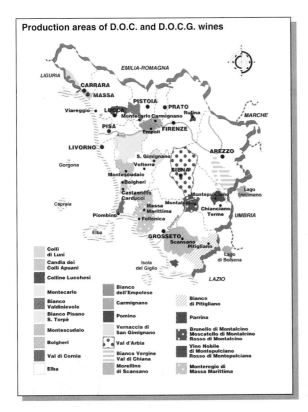

Production areas of D.O.C. and D.O.C.G. wines

Colli di Luni
Candia dei Colli Apuani
Colline Lucchesi
Montecarlo
Bianco Valdinievole
Bianco Pisano S. Torpè
Montescudaio
Bolgheri
Val di Cornia
Elba
Bianco dell'Empolese
Carmignano
Pomino
Vernaccia di San Gimignano
Val d'Arbia
Bianco Vergine Val di Chiana
Morellino di Scansano
Bianco di Pitigliano
Parrina
Brunello di Montalcino
Moscatello di Montalcino
Rosso di Montalcino
Vino Nobile di Montepulciano
Rosso di Montepulciano
Monteregio di Massa Marittima

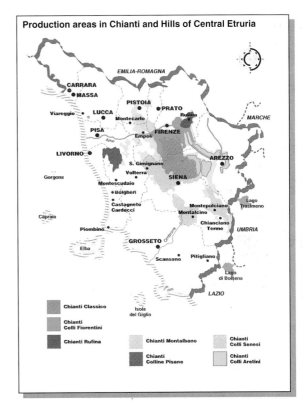

Production areas in Chianti and Hills of Central Etruria

Chianti Classico
Chianti Colli Fiorentini
Chianti Rufina
Chianti Montalbano
Chianti Colline Pisane
Chianti Colli Senesi
Chianti Colli Aretini

shrewdly managed their vines with an eye for innovation, while at the same time trying to preserve the spirit of a very long-standing tradition. The big revolution in Tuscan wine in conformity to international standards began in the hills around Bolgheri, thanks to the Marquis Mario Incisa della Rocchetta who, in the late 1960s, directed his efforts towards cultivating *cabernet sauvignon* with the aim of producing Bordeaux-style wines in the area. This is how Sassicaia was born. It is a "matrix wine" from which originate many others in the same area, including the extremely elegant Ornellaia, Masseto and Guado al Tasso of the Marquis Antinori. The native Tignanello emerged in response to these major wines. This masterpiece is made by Piero

The famous Vin Santo, made from malvasia grapes, matures in these barrels until its reaches its full alcohol content and bouquet.

Antinori from *sangiovese* grapes cultivated in Chianti and has led the producers of Chianti (a wine mentioned in 14th century documents) to renew their commitment to the promotion of a wine which, by virtue of its aroma, vitality, fragrance and longevity, is one of the most versatile reds in Italy. Montalcino is home to Sangiovese, a major red made from the large *sangiovese* grape (known locally as *brunello*). It has a unique fragrance and ages well. Vino Nobile di Montepulciano is produced from a variety of this grape called *prugnolo gentile*. It has an intense, delicate bouquet and a full, soft taste containing only the slightest hint of tannins. In Maremma, the *sangiovese* grape is used to make Morellino di Scansano, a robust, aggressive red with surprising strength which goes well with similarly strong cheeses such as Pecorino

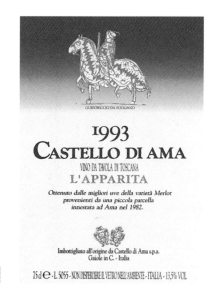

The medieval towers of San Gimignano and the Vernaccia vineyards. The wine was popular with numerous Renaissance popes.

Siciliano, Fiore Sardo or Asiago. Tuscany is certainly not the choice area for white wines. However, there are a number of interesting exceptions. Top of the list is Vernaccia di San Gimignano, a fresh, fruity wine which appears in medieval documents and was Pope Paul III's favorite; it is excellent with cheeses such as Mozzarella, Robiola or Taleggio. Vin Santo is another major Tuscan white, traditionally made from a blend of grapes (*malvasia* and *trebbiano*) which are dried on wickerwork shelves and left to age in small barrels for at least three years. It provides a good contrast to mature cheeses such as Bitto della Valtellina.

♥ Sassicaia - Tenuta San Guido Marchesi Incisa della Rocchetta
Made in Bolgheri (an area whose cypress trees were extolled by Carducci) from a blend of cabernet sauvignon grapes (70%), and cabernet franc grapes (30%), this red had a pioneering role in the change in the conception, style and image of the Italian wine industry on the world stage. Intensely fragrant and full-bodied, it is an indulgent accompaniment to Parmigiano Reggiano.

UMBRIA

Umbria is often described as being a "green" region and here, the love of nature and a tender nostalgia for the past are synthesized in a cuisine which goes straight to the heart. The simple recipes which come out of the farmyards or the fishing tradition upheld by the large fishing boats on Lake Trasimeno are enriched by the unmistakable aroma of one of the finest extra-virgin olive oils in Italy. This makes a superb accompaniment to one of the great treasures of the regional gastronomy: the famous black Norcia truffles which, unlike the

Below: The Lungarotti vineyards, in the green Torgiano countryside near Perugia.

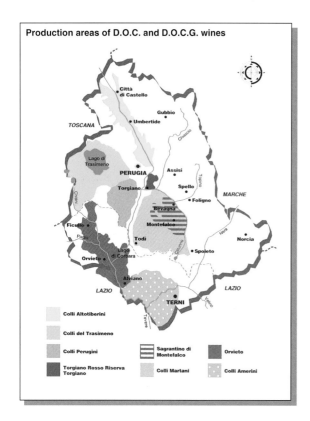

Production areas of D.O.C. and D.O.C.G. wines

TOSCANA

Città di Castello
Gubbio
Umbertide
Lago di Trasimeno
PERUGIA
Assisi
Torgiano
Spello
Foligno
MARCHE
Bevagna
Montefalco
Ficulle
Todi
Norcia
Spoleto
Orvieto
Lago di Corbara
Alviano
LAZIO
LAZIO
TERNI

Colli Altotiberini

Colli del Trasimeno

Colli Perugini

Torgiano Rosso Riserva Torgiano

Sagrantino di Montefalco

Colli Martani

Orvieto

Colli Amerini

white Alba variety, do not go with butter. Be it a simple *bruschetta* (toasted bread), stuffed pigeon, or one of the many kinds of pasta made from flour and water (*ceriole, umbrichelli, stringozzi, manfricoli*), black truffle provides the "added value" which makes the dish rise to unexpected heights of flavor. The idea that simplicity is necessarily a restriction to gastronomic pleasure is quite simply not true, as the various soups made from "humble" cereals such as spelt, or from the flavorsome DOC lentils go to show.

As for second course dishes, the classic pork recipes and pork sausages are the gastronomic mainstay (do not forget that the medieval town of Norcia is home to "norcini", one of the oldest butchers' guilds); alternatively you can choose from spicy lamb or pigeon, which are both unrivaled in their perfection.

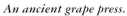

An ancient grape press.

**San Giorgio -
Cantine Lungarotti**
Pecorino Toscano

**Torgiano Rosso Vigna
Monticchio -
Cantine Lungarotti**
Provolone Valpadana

**Sagrantino di Montefalco -
A Caprai - Val di Maggio**
Castelmagno

**Cervaro della Sala -
Castello della Sala**
Toma Piemontese

**Muffato della Sala -
Castello della Sala**
Gorgonzola

**Orvieto Classico -
Decugnano dei Barbi**
Robiola di Roccaverano

*Enthusiasts of the history of
wine must stop at Torgiano,
near Perugia, to visit the
extensive museum founded by
the Lungarotti family.*

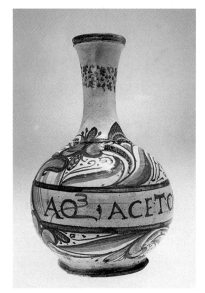
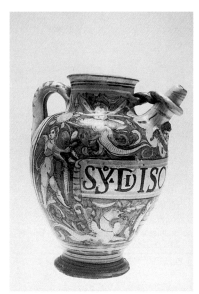

Needless to say, Umbria boasts a wine industry with a similar tradition of excellence, as a visit to Torgiano, near Perugia, readily shows. Here, the noble Graziano Baglioni palace hosts an interesting museum containing a unique collection of objects and documents on the subject of wine, under the supervision of Giorgio Lungarotti who, with his Torgiano Rubesco, became the pioneer of major wine production in Umbria.

Montefalco is the second obligatory port of call on our tour of the regional "tops". It is home to Sagrantino, a bold, powerful red, rich in tannins and with a long aftertaste, which makes a good accompaniment to cheeses like Castelmagno and Grana Padano. The town of Orvieto is home to one of the oldest and most famous Umbrian wines, produced in the shadow of the extraordinary cathedral and its rose window: Orvieto, which is pale yellow in color and has a pleasantly bitter, spicy taste. It complements Taleggio or Quartirolo well, and in its best vintages provides an effective contrast to the strong, creamy flavor of Gorgonzola. Finally, mention must go to the Marquis Antinori at Castello della Sala, home to one of the most interesting Italian Chardonnays, the sunny and fresh Cervaro, as well as Muffato, a dense, elegant and succulent wine with a taste of ripe fruit which stands comparison to the major French Sauternes: in short, an original masterpiece which goes well with very mature cheeses such as Fiore Sardo.

Castello della Sala, near Ficulle. Its vineyards produce Cervaro, one of the finest Italian whites.

♥ *Cervaro della Sala - Castello della Sala*
The "white cousin" of the famous red Sassicaia, this wine is responsible for the continued growth in the quality of Italian whites, through modernization of the production process, accentuation and improvement of the combination of local grapes and the successful blending of these with the finest in the world. A careful blend of Chardonnay grapes and Grechetto grapes, it boasts a bouquet and a palate which are both rich and elegant.

LAZIO

From the Trimalcione banquet to the luxury of the *dolce vita*, to the gastronomic orgies enjoyed by the patriarchal families in the Castelli, the cuisine in Lazio has a reputation for being heavy, domestic and ostentatious. It consists of clear, decisive flavors which evoke the countryside where sheep still graze among the ancient aqueducts, and it leaves no room for dietary compromise. In reality, Roman cuisine is a blend of three very different traditions: the opulence of the popes and cardinals, the Jewish cuisine of the old Ghetto area

Below: the Frascati vineyards in a landscape popular with 19th - century artists.

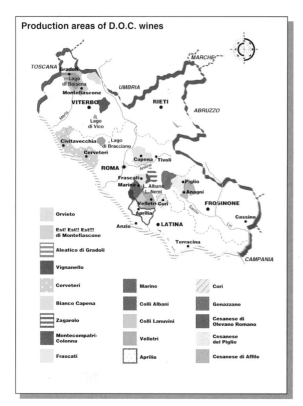

Production areas of D.O.C. wines

Orvieto

Est! Est!! Est!!! di Montefiascone

Aleatico di Gradoli

Vignanello

Cerveteri

Bianco Capena

Zagarolo

Montecompatri-Colonna

Frascati

Marino

Colli Albani

Colli Lanuvini

Velletri

Aprilia

Cori

Genazzano

Cesanese di Olevano Romano

Cesanese del Piglio

Cesanese di Affile

(where one can sample such original combinations as fried cod fillets and artichokes, soup made from ray fish and broccoli, or moist ricotta cake), and the popular, rustic tradition. This is the land of roast lamb and pork. Popular too is *quinto quarto*, left over parts of the meat poorer used in rich dishes such as *rigatoni* with *pajata* (a sauce made from the entrails of suckling calf).

CASTEL DE PAOLIS

Frascati

Denominazione di Origine Controllata

SUPERIORE

CASTEL DE PAOLIS

I Quattro Mori

The faithful exponents of this kind of cuisine live in Sabina to the east, or Ciociaria to the south, home to the most famous dishes in the capital, including the Roman "number one":

Favorite Wines

Est! Est!! Est!!! Poggio dei Gelsi - Cantina Falesco
Mozzarella di Bufala Campana

Montiano - Cantina Falesco
Caciocavallo Silano

Frascati Superiore Vigna Adriana - Castel de' Paolis
Bra Tenero

Quattro Mori - Castel de' Paolis
Montasio

Torre Ercolana - Colacicchi
Ragusano

These bunches of trebbiano grapes are used to produce the famous Est! Est!! Est!!! from Montefiascone.

This old print illustrates the medieval story of a German canon who sent a servant on ahead of him. Where the wine was good, the servant was instructed to write "Est" (which meant "there is" in latin) on the tavern. But in Montefiascone the wine was so good that he had to write "Est! Est!! Est!!!".

♥ Frascati Superiore - Castel de' Paolis

It took the intelligence and patience of Giulio Santarelli, long-standing political activist, to rediscover and promote a white wine with exceptional potential, but which had fallen into disrepute. It is made from a complex blend of malvasia puntinata, bellone, cacchione, trebbiano giallo, bonvino, grechetto, passerina and vermentina grapes, and is the product of hard labor in both the vineyards and the cellars. The result? A fine balance of strength, body and complexity which goes well with a mild Taleggio.

amatriciana, pasta with crispy bacon, tomato and Pecorino. Extolled by tourists and by the cinema during the boom years of Cinecittà, in reality the wines of Lazio are still subject to an unwise "quantitative" production policy which has been followed for many years by producers concerned only with easy sales. However, the general renewal of the Italian wine industry has prompted some producers to come up with really high-quality products. Beginning with the Viterbo area, Est! Est!! Est!!! is worth a mention: fresh and palatable, it is an undemanding white. Montiano is an extremely interesting albeit unpretentions house wine. Like Est! Est!! Est!!!, it is made in Montefiascone from the blend of *merlot* and *cabernet* grapes used in the production of Bordeaux wines. These days, however, many new things are also happening to the classic Frascati, an agreeably concentrated, full-bodied wine which goes well with cheeses such as Pecorino, especially if they are not too mature.

THE MARCHES

This region boasts one of the richest and most interesting seafood cuisines in Italy; one only has to think of *brodetto*, the famous fish soup flavored with onion, for this to be apparent. Every tiny port is home to a different recipe and infinite "trade secrets", ranging from the use of saffron to the thickening effect of scorpion fish on broth. In general, in the fish-based cuisine of the Marches, seafood products and the fruits of the land are readily combined. Cheese is used to stuff cuttlefish, ham pairs with red mullet in a recipe which is used all along the coast, while a blend of garlic, aromatic herbs (marjoram in particular) and breadcrumbs

Favorite Wines

***Verdicchio di Matelica -
La Monacesca***
*Mozzarella di Bufala
Campana*

***Rosso Conero Dorico -
Moroder***
Casciotta di Urbino

la Monacesca

VERDICCHIO
DI MATELICA
*Denominazione
di Origine
Controllata*

75 cl.   1995   13% vol

*The production of superior
wines in the Marches dates
back to the Middle Ages.*

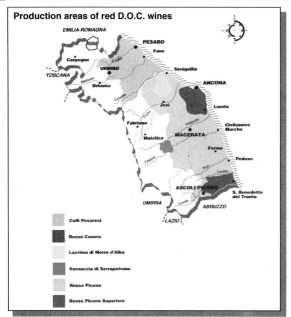

Production areas of red D.O.C. wines

- Colli Pesaresi
- Rosso Conero
- Lacrima di Morro d'Alba
- Vernaccia di Serrapetrona
- Rosso Piceno
- Rosso Piceno Superiore

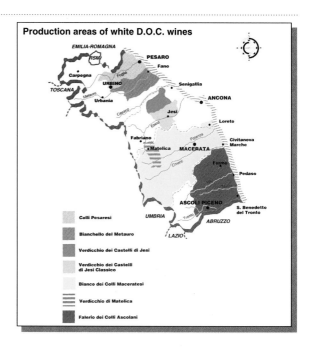

Production areas of white D.O.C. wines

- Colli Pesaresi
- Bianchello del Metauro
- Verdicchio dei Castelli di Jesi
- Verdicchio dei Castelli di Jesi Classico
- Bianco dei Colli Maceratesi
- Verdicchio di Matelica
- Falerio dei Colli Ascolani

is frequently the basic ingredient in the preparation of grilled fish, giving it its special flavor.

The pasta course is dominated by *vincisgrassi*, a 17th-century imperial lasagne made from a rich layering of giblets, mushrooms, béchamel sauce and sweetbreads, and *passatelli*, a soup made from small, soft gnocchi, echoing the Romagna cuisine. Second course dishes often make use of *potacchio*, a sauce which adds flavor to chicken, rabbit and even fried fish. The white Acqualagna truffle – one of the most sought-after in Italy – gives a touch of refinement to many dishes. However, the ultimate in culinary pleasure is to be found in the classic stuffed and fried olives called *olive all'ascolana*, thought to date back to the ancient people of Piceno.

Two major wines – both in a state of continued growth and development – are produced in the Marches. These are Verdicchio in both of its denominations: Castelli di Jesi e di Matelica and Rosso Conero. The amphora-shaped bottles in which it was marketed and which guaranteed its success have now been abandoned and Verdicchio is being relaunched.

Castelli di Jesi produces a Verdicchio which goes nicely with fish, but also with cheeses such as Taleggio and Robiola.

A white wine with a strong bouquet, it has a gentle, long-lasting taste. It makes a good accompaniment to Mozzarella di Bufala Campana. Rosso Conero is a balanced wine with a seductive aroma and an elegant taste. It is the ideal accompaniment to Casciotta di Urbino, but it also goes well with stronger cheeses such as Raschera.

♥ *Rosso Conoro Dorico - Alessandro Moroder*
Intelligent young producer Alessandro Moroder knows what he is about. His red is made from montepulciano grapes and allowed to mature only for a short time in barrels. It has body, fullness, balance, class, and elegance. It is a wine that ages well and goes nicely with Asiago.

ABRUZZO AND MOLISE

Favorite Wines

Trebbiano d'Abruzzo - Valentini
Quartirolo

Montepulciano d'Abruzzo - Valentini
Pecorino Toscano

Biferno Rosso Ramitello - Di Majo Norante
Provolone Valpadana

The Abruzzo, an interesting region whose unusual geography creates a clear division between coast and mountains, boasts a rich gastronomic tradition. Until the end of the last century it was home to the famous Villa Santa Maria School which fostered a host of cooks who then emigrated to the best courts and restaurants in the world to become ambassadors of the delicious flavors of Italian cuisine. Its dishes are decisive, robust and boosted by the use of spices. Of these, chili is the most common. *Panarda* is still a thriving tradition in this region, an unending procession of dishes, from the delicious Campotosto *mortadella* to boiled meats, soups to boiled lamb, home-made pasta to a range of desserts: *torroni* (nougat) and sweets made from almonds, including the famous coated almonds made in

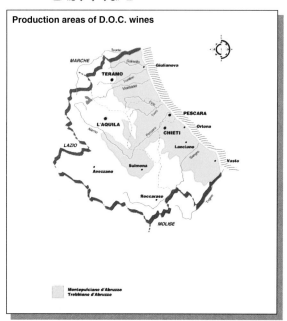

Production areas of D.O.C. wines

Montepulciano d'Abruzzo
Trebbiano d'Abruzzo

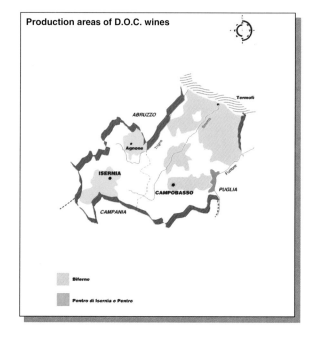

Production areas of D.O.C. wines

Biferno

Pentro di Isernia o Pentro

Sulmona which are unrivaled in Italy. Don't miss the *maccheroni alla chitarra* (flat spaghetti), so called because they are produced using a special utensil made from steel strings (hence the name "guitar").

The symbol of Teramo, the gastronomic capital, is more complex: soup "of the virtues" made from a rich blend of vegetables and prized parts of pig. The coastal cuisine also has much to offer, including a rich fish soup. Chili features in another specialty of the area, *scapece* (made from fish which has been left to mature in terracotta containers with salt and saffron), and in a recipe with angler fish, which is prepared with anchovy fillets to give it added flavor.

The cuisine in Molise is more spartan and rustic. *Crejoli, laganelle, sagne,* and *taccozze* are among the numerous pasta dishes which are usually served with a lamb or mutton sauce, or with turnip-tops or beans fried with bacon and a pinch of chili. The soups are also good, such as *risciusce* (a mix of cereals) and *lacci e patate* (celery and potato), typical of the Campobasso area.

Second course dishes are also characterized by strong flavors which have their roots in the pastoral tradition. *Pezzata,* a

mutton-based dish with tomato, rosemary and chili, is excellent, as is baby goat with peppers. However, the real triumph of the imagination comes in the form of tripe, which is prepared in a thousand different ways: from *allulere* (in which the tripe is used to stuff lamb) to *torcinelli* (a sort of parcel made from lamb's entrails and stuffed with tripe).

In Abruzzo and Molise, the onshore wind and the protective mountain range provide favorable climatic conditions for viticulture. It was no accident that, in Roman times, these areas produced *Praetutian,* a well-reputed red. Since those glorious days, regional production has been through a number of phases, including that of secretly supplying strong wines to fake the more noble wines from the North. However, producers and the cooperatives are trying hard to come up with quality products made from local grape varieties (don't forget that Loreto Aprutino is home to Edoardo Valentini, who is responsible for producing some of the best wines in the country): from Trebbiano Bianco to the warm and fragrant Montepulciano, to Biferno (the only DOC in Molise other than Pentro di Isernia).

Trebbiano d'Abruzzo - Edoardo Valentini
The Valentini family has owned land and been producing wine since 1650. Their white (one of the most unusual and long-lived in Italy), made exclusively from trebbiano grapes, is notable for its strength and impact. It has a lovely golden color and a full, elegant bouquet of fruit and spices with hints of coffee and chocolate. It complements a mild Valpadana Provolone nicely.

APULIA

The cuisine in Apulia is a medley of exotic Mediterranean flavors based on extra-virgin olive oil, pasta, vegetables and fish. Seafood is a true religion. Frequently, it is simply served raw, but it also features in a number of delicious recipes, ranging from the classic spaghetti with sea urchins to the more elaborate *tiella* (a throwback to the period of Spanish influence and the tradition of *paella*), made from rice, mussels and potatoes. Pasta, such as *orecchiette* (almost always served with turnip-tops) and *cavatieddi*, a kind of hollow cylinder which is accompanied by a sauce made from baby tomatoes, celery and basil and topped with a generous sprinkling of grated Pecorino, are two classic dishes. Second course dishes are mainly fish-based. Specialties include baked anchovies with

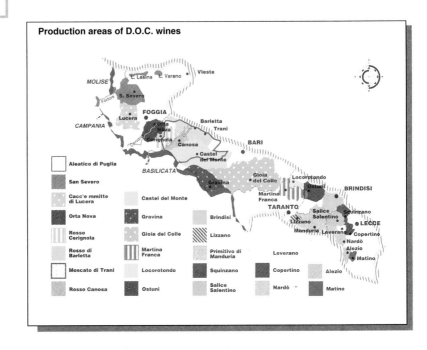

Production areas of D.O.C. wines

The harvest and pressing of the grapes have always been critical stages in the production of a fine wine.

breadcrumbs and Pecorino, and *orata alla barese* (cooked in wine with parsnips, herbs and rasins), although meat – and particularly lamb – is used in a number of delicious recipes. Eggplant is at the heart of the regional cuisine, and is prepared in many different ways: roasted with garlic, mint and herbs; stuffed with capers, olives and anchovies and baked in the oven; and *alla Sant'Oronzo*, the patron of Lecce (in reality a variation on the classic "parmigiana").

The characteristic trulli in a landscape dominated by vines.

♥ *Brindisi Rosso Patriglione - Cosimo Taurino*

This is a complex and unusual red, made from the late harvest of negroamaro grapes and a small percentage of malvasia nera grapes. It is certainly not the best red wine to come out of the South, but it is definitely the most popular (of the quality wines at least). The combination of assertiveness, concentration, vigor, and alcohol, and its complex structure, strike the palate forcefully. It has a deep orange color and an exceptionally powerful bouquet, while its high alcohol content gives it the balanced taste of a liqueur. It goes well with a very mature Pecorino Siciliano.

The vineyards, together with the olive groves, are a characteristic feature of the regional landscape. With an annual output of twelve million hectoliters, Apulia qualifies as one of the main wine regions in Italy, a fact which explains why so many wines have become "blending" products, especially in the past. Here too, however, a number of venturesome producers are trying to bring out the potential of a region whose wine-making tradition goes back centuries. The most interesting wines from this region are undoubtedly Castel del Monte (named after the famous castle belonging to Federico II), the white Gravina, the fragrant, dry and delicate Locorotondo, Salice Salentino (notable both in its red and rosé form) and the strong Primitivo di Manduria, a red which easily "hits" the 14% mark and is an ideal accompaniment to very mature cheeses.

CAMPANIA

The cuisine in Campania (and in Naples, its culinary capital) plays on the delicate balance between the muted quiet of the palaces where food is a feast for the eyes as well as for the stomach, and the din in the narrow alleyways smelling of ragout and fried food. Thus, on the one hand there are the pompous and delicious recipes prepared by the "monzù" (as the cooks employed by the aristocratic families used to be called) for their masters, such as *sartù* and *timballo*, while on the other there is the world of the "lazzeri", the sansculottes and the plebeian philosophers.

The region is the pasta capital of Italy and the complex first course dishes range from *spaghetti* to *ziti*, *perciatelli* to *paccheri*. Tomatoes (the insuperable Sanmarzano or the flavorsome "cherry" varieties) provide the common element throughout.

It is hard not to be tempted by

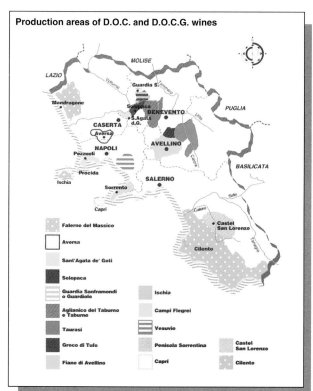

Production areas of D.O.C. and D.O.C.G. wines

MOLISE

LAZIO

Mondragone

Guardia S.

BENEVENTO

PUGLIA

Solopaca

S.Agata d.G.

CASERTA

Aversa

AVELLINO

NAPOLI

Pozzuoli

BASILICATA

Procida

SALERNO

Ischia

Sorrento

Capri

Castel San Lorenzo

Cilento

Falerno del Massico

Aversa

Sant'Agata de' Goti

Solopaca

Guardia Sanframondi o Guardiolo

Ischia

Aglianico del Taburno e Taburno

Campi Flegrei

Taurasi

Vesuvio

Greco di Tufo

Penisola Sorrentina

Castel San Lorenzo

Fiano di Avellino

Capri

Cilento

The Irpinia vineyards produce some of the finest "crus" in Campania.

Mastroberardino

Only aging in barrels for the correct length of time can give the wine bouquet and refinement.

the fried-food shops with their savory *pizzelle* and rice balls or sweet *zeppole* and *graffe*. But it is the fish-vegetable-starch trio that lies at the heart of a cuisine which, in Campania, was "Mediterranean" even before this term entered into everyday speech. Sea, sun and kitchen gardens take pride of place in a culinary tradition whose flavors beg to be enjoyed to the full, be it in *parmigiana di melanzane*, a flavorsome stir-fry, an exciting soup made from vegetables and pork, or even *palatella*, a simple loaf rubbed with garlic and filled with mozzarella, tomato and basil (one of the winning trios in another mainstay of the

regional cuisine: pizza). The climate in Campania is ideal for viticulture – it is not by chance that the Romans used to call the region "felix". Over time, however, the wine industry has seen a general decline and today only a few leading producers are able to make quality products – and this in spite of the fact that, in contrast to the North where many white grape varieties have had to be imported (*chardonnay* for example), this terrain has been home to vines such as *falanghina*, *biancolella*, *greco* and *fiano* for centuries.
In conclusion, mention must go to the age-old and famous

Greco di Tufo, red Gragnano, the scented and aromatic wines of the island of Ischia and the harmonious Fiano di Avellino, which is an ideal accompaniment to Mozzarella. Regional production is almost exclusively white; but it is home to one fine red, Montevetrano, made in the Salerno region from a blend of *cabernet sauvignon*, *merlot* and the local *aglianico* grapes.

The famous and ancient Greco is produced in these vineyards.

♥ ***Montevetrano - Montevetrano***
Photographer Silvia Imparato turned to wine-making towards the end of the 1980s. Thanks to the assistance of wine guru Riccardo Cotarella, she has enjoyed almost immediate success, to the extent that the renowned American wine critic Robert Parker awarded her red of '93 an outstanding 96/100. Made from cabernet sauvignon (the classic Bordeaux grape variety) and a small amount of local aglianico grapes, it is a dense red with a full, balanced bouquet, fine body and a fruity taste. It goes well with a classic Fontina from the Valle d'Aosta.

BASILICATA AND CALABRIA

From kitchen gardens to urban courtyards, to harsh mountain landscapes, Basilicata is characterized by the deep-rooted flavors of the countryside. Here cattle are scarce, and so sheep farming naturally prevails. Grilled mutton cooked with a generous helping of garlic was once a classic delicacy. Here pasta is a very serious business, and there are numerous specialties: *maccheroni col ferretto* and

Production areas of D.O.C. wines

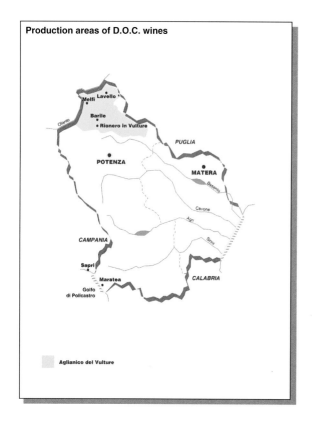

Aglianico del Vulture

Production areas of D.O.C. wines

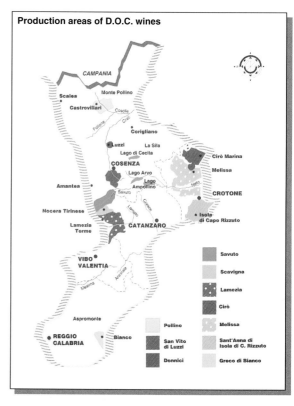

Savuto

Scavigna

Lamezia

Cirò

Pollino

San Vito di Luzzi

Donnici

Melissa

Sant'Anna di Isola di C. Rizzuto

Greco di Bianco

*Many cellars are housed in ancient dwellings in Basilicata, an
agricultural region which produces strong wines.*

strascinati (made using a
rectangular wooden utensil
called a "cavarola" which gives
the pasta the grooves that allow
it to retain a coating of sauce).
Pork also plays an important role
in the regional cuisine:
remember that the famous
"lucanica" does not come from
the North, but from these valleys,
as the Latin writer Terenzio
Varrone relates, underlining the
fact that it was here that the
Roman legions learned the
secrets of making tasty sausages.
Calabria also has a clearly-
defined cuisine. In this region,
the sauces are made using
generous amounts of chili, or
traditional recipes such as the
characteristic *'nduia*, making use
of cheap cuts of pork to flavor
first course dishes. However, the
sea also plays an important role
here, and there are a number of
recipes which make use of the
excellent but often undervalued
pesce azzurro, or swordfish,
from the Straights of Messina.
As for the wine industry, the two
regions are trying hard to bring
themselves into line with the
process of national renewal. In
Lucania, the only DOC of any
worth is Aglianico del Vulture, a
full-bodied red with a rich

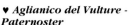

bouquet and considerable strength. The Ionian coast in the center of Calabria is home to Cirò, a wine which is equally interesting in its red, white and rosé form. Sila and Aspromonte also produce good wines, although it is to the south coast that we must look to find an extremely interesting dessert wine, Greco di Bianco, which is rich and honeyed, ideal to accompany Gorgonzola or a mature Ragusano. Praise must also go to the estates which have had the courage to combine traditional and less typical grape varieties, producing real masterpieces such as Gravello, made from a blend of *gaglioppo* and *cabernet sauvignon grapes.*

♥ *Aglianico del Vulture - Paternoster*

A kind of southern Barolo, this classic red with a deep purple color is made exclusively from aglianico grapes and is the pride of production in Luca. It is a noble wine, strong and yet well-balanced, captivating and fruity, and the finest vintages are long-lived. It has a full bouquet with a pleasant hint of strawberries and a distinct and long-lasting taste, making it an ideal accompaniment to Canestrato from Apulia.

SICILY

Languid, sensual, exotic; Sicilian cuisine boasts a fascinating range of flavors which reflect the cultural diversity of an island whose history goes back thousands of years. The influence of the Arab culture is apparent in a whole range of dishes: sorbets, ice-creams, *cassata cubbaita* (the delicious *torrone* made from a blend of honey and sesame).

The Greeks are present in the importance attributed to the sun and in the cultivation of olives, the Byzantines in the love of *bottarga* and strong cheeses, and the Swabians in the predilection for roasted meats. A special vote of thanks must also go to the Spanish viceroys responsible for the importation from the Balearic islands of fennel.

It is easy to see how each part of

Favorite Wines

Duca Enrico - Duca di Salaparuta
Pecorino Siciliano

Chardonnay - Tasca d'Almerita Regaleali
Toma Piemontese

Moscato di Pantelleria Bukkuram - M. De Bartoli
Formaggio di Fossa

Marsala Superiore Targa - Florio
Gorgonzola

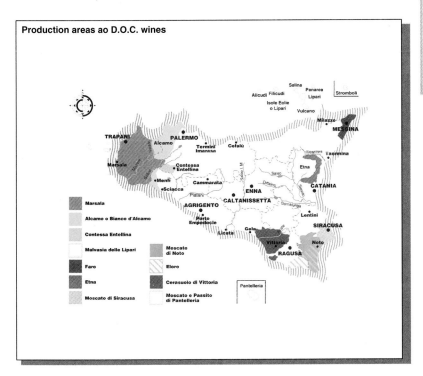

Production areas ao D.O.C. wines

Marsala

Alcamo o Bianco d'Alcamo

Contessa Entellina

Malvasia delle Lipari

Faro

Etna

Moscato di Siracusa

Moscato di Noto

Eloro

Cerasuolo di Vittoria

Moscato e Passito di Pantelleria

The English discovered Marsala at the beginning of the last century as a delicious alternative to Sherry.

Casa Florio has such a long and eventful history that it would be possible to write a kind of Sicilian "Falcon Crest" about it.

this island has developed its own cuisine from a range of unbeatable products, such as swordfish from the Straights of Messina, tuna from the Egadi islands, the citrus fruits of Paternò, the pork from Chiaramonte and the mushrooms from the forests on the slopes of Etna. As though this were not enough, even the bread and the desserts in this region are perfect.

The Sicilian wine-producing area is the largest in the country, and the amount of wine produced is proportionately large. However, there are still only a few outstanding wines, partly because of a production policy which values profit over and above quality and innovation. Of course, there are exceptions: Duca di Salaparuta (owned by the regional authorities) and Regaleali are two major estates which have respectively made their names with the exceptional and innovative Duca Enrico, a strong red which goes well with aristocratic cheeses such as Parmigiano, and the rich, sunny, elegant Chardonnay.

In addition to the interesting wines produced in the Etna area, Sicily is also home to some fine dessert wines which are ideal to accompany cheeses such as Gorgonzola and other strong cheeses: Marsala, Moscato di Pantelleria and Malvasia from the Aeolian Islands.

♥ Cabernet Sauvignon - Tasca d'Almerita Regaleali
This fine red is produced on the chalk and clay terrain of hills near Palermo. Its rich bouquet results from the twelve month aging process in barrels. The wine reflects the opulence of the grapes, the Sicilian sun and the ongoing aging process after bottling. Dark red, almost black in color, and boasting a full and complex bouquet, it is a fruity wine which is rich and elegant on the palate. It goes well with a mature Bitto della Valtellina.

Inzolia grapes, used to make the splendid Bianca di Valguarnera.

A bunch of red cappuccio grapes, which play an important role in the production of the finest reds on the island.

SARDINIA

It is a mistake to confuse Sardinian cuisine with the *linguine* in lobster sauce enjoyed by VIPs on the Smeralda Coast. You must make your way inland along the tortuous roads scented with myrtle and lentisk to discover a rustic cuisine which seems as though it has come out of a page of Homer. Here bread is of prime importance and comes in a variety of different forms. Sardinia is home to the impalpable and crunchy *carta da musica* and also to *civarzu*, the thick *focaccia* from Campidano.

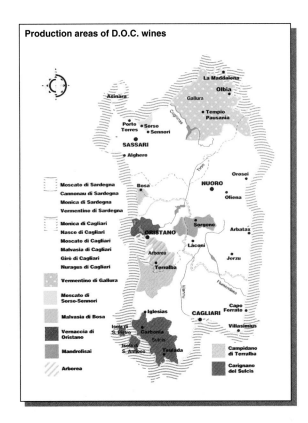

Production areas of D.O.C. wines

- Moscato di Sardegna
- Cannonau di Sardegna
- Monica di Sardegna
- Vermentino di Sardegna

- Monica di Cagliari
- Nasco di Cagliari
- Moscato di Cagliari
- Malvasia di Cagliari
- Girò di Cagliari
- Nuragus di Cagliari

- Vermentino di Gallura

- Moscato di Sorso-Sennori

- Malvasia di Bosa

- Vernaccia di Oristano

- Mandrolisai

- Arborea

- Campidano di Terralba

- Carignano del Sulcis

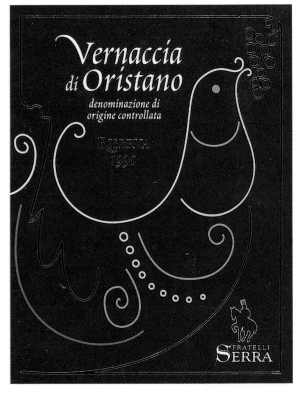

Vernaccia di Oristano
denominazione di origine controllata
RISERVA 1990
FRATELLI SERRA

The Argiolas cellars at Serdiana, near Cagliari.

MONICA DI SARDEGNA
DENOMINAZIONE DI ORIGINE CONTROLLATA

NURAGUS DI CAGLIARI
DENOMINAZIONE DI ORIGINE CONTROLLATA

VERNACCIA DI ORISTANO
DENOMINAZIONE DI ORIGINE CONTROLLATA

Bran is another important staple in the Sardinian diet. It is used to make *culingiones*, the characteristic *ravioli*, and *malloreddus*, small, grooved *gnocchi* which are enhanced with saffron in the classic version of the dish.

In the Nuoro area, the cuisine is characterized by rustic, pork-based dishes such as the delicious *porcetto*, flavored with myrtle, while in Barbagia you can still find *ghisau* in which mutton is cooked for hours.

Of note among the fish dishes are *scabecciu* (fried bogue with a vinegar marinade), *merka del Sinis* (gray mullet wrapped in swamp grass and boiled in salty water) and *aragosta all'algherese* (lobster with tomatoes and onions). Finally, on the dessert front, mention must be made of the famous almond and sugar combinations, and of the age-old *sebadas*, made from fried

Vermentino grapes are used to make the finest whites in Sardinia.

cheese and honey. Sardinian wines display something of the complex cultural stratification of the island. The white Vermentino is undoubtedly reminiscent of the Genovese tradition, while Vernaccia di Oristano comes from the Romans (although legend has it that it originated in the tears shed by Saint Giusta di Otoca over the destruction of Campidano) and Torbato di Alghero from the Catalan Tubat.

The region is home to numerous other white wines, from the ancient Nuragus di Cagliari to Vermentino di Sardinia, Vermentino di Gallura and Vernaccia di Oristano. The reds are dominated by the strong Cannonau, which is a perfect accompaniment to the two local cheeses and is made from the same grape variety as an exceptional modern wine, Turriga, from the Antonio Argiolas estate.

♥ Cannonau di Sardegna Costera - Antonio Argiolas

It is largely thanks to the Argiolas brothers that the wine industry in Sardinia has improved and can now boast some quality products. This white was once considered dense and heavy – in short, the antithesis of elegance, immediacy and smoothness. However, the "inventor" of Sassicaia, Giacomo Tachis, has managed to soften and refine a product which is part of the natural patrimony of this marvelous region. Cannonau di Argiolas is ruby red in color and has a musty bouquet with a hint of spices. It is an inviting wine with a gentle, balanced taste, making it an excellent accompaniment to Grana Padano.

Paolo Scotto

CHEESE AND WINE OF ITALY

With the collaboration of the
Istituto Europeo di Design
Rome

GREMESE

ACKNOWLEDGEMENTS
The Publisher and the Author wish to thank the trade consortia and wine and cheese producers who supplied many of the illustrations.
Special thanks also go to chef Antonello Colonna, maître fromager Alberto Marcomini of Venice, Emilio Volpetti of the excellent delicatessen on Via Marmorata in Rome, and Fabio Turchetti of "L'Espresso" guide.
Special thanks also to Franco Ricci, editor-in-chief of Il Sommelier Italiano *and the Italian Sommelier Association from whose lovely book all the maps of regional wines of Denominated Origin were taken.*

A special thanks to Istituto Europeo di Design in Rome and to Antonio Barrella and Vitaliano Lopez who co-ordinated the photography work of Davide Monteleone, Federica Rosa, Alessandra Manca, Fabio Cuttiga, Elena Cornalis mentioned below.

Original title : Formaggi e Vini d'Italia
© 1997 Gremese Editore S.r.l.

Translated from the Italian by : Lenor Rosenberg

Editor : Laura Clarke

Cover by : Carlo Soldatini

Photographs by: Giorgio De Camillis (p.p. 9, 11, 17, 23, 32, 35, 40, 41, 45, 47, 53, 55, 56, 58, 59, 61, 62, 64, 66, 67, 69); Davide Monteleone (p. 19); Federica Rosa (p. 27); Alessandra Manca (p.p. 29, 31, 33 bottom, 43 top, 65, 70); Fabio Cuttiga (p. 50); Elena Cornalis (p. 60). All the other photographs were kindly supplied by the consortia and producers whom we thank.

Photocomposition and photolithography : Gescom S.r.l. - Viterbo

Printed and bound by: Grafedit S.p.a. - Bergamo

GREMESE
First Edition © 1999
New Books s.r.l.
Via Virginia Agnelli, 88 - 00151 Rome
Tel.: +39/06 65740507 Fax: +39/06 65740509
E-mail: gremese@gremese.com
website: http://www.gremese.com

ISBN 88-7301-301-5

CONTENTS

PREFACE

*T*hese days, eating "light" is in. With every passing day, a growing number of people are converted to the "religion" of the Mediterranean diet. Of course we are all for a diet based on the aroma of extra-virgin olive oil, fish, legumes, green vegetables, and pasta. The problem, however, is far more intricate than that. Medical science's attack on the pleasures of eating has brought about a profound revolution in habits and customs, creating a new relationship with food. People have learned that, even in terms of prevention, there is a close connection between health and what one eats. That's why, with time, they have turned to products and recipes that pay careful attention to the nutritional value of food. The food industry could certainly not let an opportunity like that go to waste. It threw all its weight behind the philosophy of healthy eating and rapidly took over the market with a series of new products that judiciously count fat and calories. Looked at one way, this concern is praiseworthy, but considering that the natural flavors of many foods might well be lost with time, it is also a shame.

The heart of this revolution in food is found in the deep changes in the meaning we give to the iniquities of the palate. As our original values progressively vanish, these transgressions have been transformed from a venal sin into a hideous crime against our health. Although the new nutritional imperatives certainly promise us a longer, less troubled life - maybe - little attention is paid to the hedonistic aspect of food and its liturgy. The result - just to give one obvious example - is that the information about the oft demonized cholesterol and its suspected terrible effects on the cardio-vascular system has negatively affected our attitude towards many products - principally butter and cheese - often becoming a sort of unconscious deterrent. This is utterly ridiculous, not only from a gastronomic but also from a medical point of view. When all these products are part of a well-balanced diet, they are salutary for the body which benefits from the contribution of proteins and minerals. Hence the notion of a brief journey through the cheeses of Italy, their history and the many traditions and recipes that tie them so closely to the culture and history of a specific region. This needs doing before the fusion between the new fanaticism over health and a misunderstanding of industrial progress leads to a general leveling of taste. Discovering - or rediscovering - the vast range of flavors of Italy's cheeses, from the austere Piedmontese Castelmagno of to the enchanting Casciotta of Urbino, becomes an act of culinary creativity. While we have no intention of falling back on the rhetoric of "the good food of the old days", before our abdication to vacuum packs, microwaves, sushi or chefs' more or less nouvelle eccentricities, it would be very sad to forget what Pecorino tastes like.

INTRODUCTION

*T*he French take cheese very seriously, so seriously in fact that it is as important a chapter in the nation's gastronomic history as wine. There are specialized shops in every town selling the products of the various regions in their varying stages of maturing, from the creamy Reblochon to the green-veined Roquefort. In Italy, on the other hand, aside from praiseworthy attempts to salvage the situation, there is no enlightened culture of cheese consumption. Proof of this is found in restaurants where, in the vast majority of cases, the mediocre selection is disgraceful. Starting from this observation, I thought it would be entertaining to write a sort of catalog of the palate, one that described Italian cheeses without being too specialized or abstruse. While many of these cheeses are of extraordinary quality, they are practically unknown outside the area where they are produced. This is a great shame because a large number of cheeses could enrich our daily diet with numerous recipes, ideas and tastes.

The first problem was deciding what criterion to use when choosing from among the 400 or so types of cheese listed in Italy, proof of the wealth and vitality of the cheese-making tradition. Finally, the simplest way, and one also in keeping with the spirit of the Maastricht Treaty, seemed to be to consider the products which, for their quality, tradition and uniform standards, already have the label proving protected origin. The PDO (Protected Denomination of Origin) was created by the European Union as a consumer protection standard. However, since all good rules mean exceptions, I decided to add two remarkable cheeses which it would have been a crime to exclude. That's why Bagòss and Formaggio di Fossa were included in this list which starts in Valle d'Aosta and descends towards the south, ending up in Sardinia. In order to make it as practical as possible, a recipe is also included for most cheeses. Most are regional specialities, but I also wanted to present a few creative exceptions. And here the contribution of Antonello Colonna, chef of Labico, a characteristic medieval hamlet south of Rome, was irreplaceable. Colonna is well known to Italy's TV audiences for his tasty recipes which he presents along with Rosanna Lambertucci on the popular show Più sani più belli *(The healthier you are, the better you look). Antonello Colonna loves a good challenge - it is no coincidence that he was the 1990 World Cup chef. He invested a great deal of effort in respecting original regional tastes, while taking care that the recipes (for four people, unless stated otherwise) are easy to follow by the inexperienced. The result is an epicurean excursion through the many typical dishes of our regional culinary traditions as well as an enjoyable opportunity to add cheese to our daily diet.*

And since the pleasure of Bacchus should always accompany the joy of food, the description of each cheese has been enriched with some suggestions from the other volume in this two-volume set, which focuses on the wines of Italy. Much has been written on how to pair food and wine. There are no scientific rules, and room should be left for personal taste, however arbitrary and strange it may seem. Without being too conditioned by academic standards, I have chosen the wines "closest to my heart", using classic accompaniments as well as a little provocation here and there. Wines are given without the best vintage - this is certainly a limitation - but the idea was to try and avoid weighing down the text, trusting in the reader's common sense and love of experimentation. In order to create some sort of "framework" for pairing, an excellent way to start is to try a typical wine of the region where the cheese we are tasting is produced. Be that as it may, the reader should remember that the wine's purpose is to give harmony to the taste of

the cheese and to prolong the pleasure of the taste in one's mouth, whether the accompanying wine "supports" the taste or "contrasts" it. A matured Castelmagno, for example, needs a full-bodied red like a Barbaresco, whereas a Taleggio would go down better with fresh whites with delicate bouquets. The very same Castelmagno can become sublime when combined with a Moscato Passito from Pantelleria. With Mozzarella, the classic spumante *is a perfect choice (but try* spumante *with Parmigiano Reggiano or Grana Padano as a contrast), while with Gorgonzola, despite many suggestions for a fairly full-bodied red wine, a glass of Picolit or Marsala Vergine is much more satisfying.*

The possible combinations are innumerable and the only limit is your imagination. The important thing is to learn and try...

FONTINA

Valle d'Aosta is the region of high mountains, the breathtaking valleys of Mont Blanc, Monte Rosa and Matterhorn. You can travel along the pathways of the Gran Paradiso National Park through a succession of uncontaminated landscapes, amidst flowers and animals. It is an ecological revival of the routes so dear to King Victor Emanuel II, the "Hunter King". "Alpine" is a term that also applies perfectly to Fontina, one of Italy's oldest, most famous cheeses, as well as the uncrossed star of regional cuisine. It is no accident that, in 1477, Pantaleone da Confienza, physician of Vercelli, who edited for the Duke of Savoy what could be considered a first example of those gourmet's guides so popular today, wrote that, in Valle d'Aosta, "the cheeses are good and the pastures excellent." The actual name *Fontina,* however, appears for the first time in a document of 1717, in the papers of the inexhaustible archives of the Ospizio del Gran San Bernardo.

No one has been able to establish the definitive origin of the name of this noble cheese: according to some it comes from the summer pasture of Fontin in the commune of Quart; others link it to the tiny village of Fontinaz; and still others think it carries the last name of an ancient family of cheese-makers, or that its tendency to melt, or *fondere* in Italian, influenced its name with time.

The main ingredient of Fontina is the milk of two typical species of Valle d'Aosta cows, the spotted red and the spotted black. They give a superb milk whose particularly rich flavor is due to the quality of the pasturage, which benefits from the special microclimate created by the mountain barrier. Between May and September the cows graze in pastures 3000 meters above sea level on rich mountain grass (and in winter, to keep up standards, the cows are fed mountain hay and not industrial fodder). Production calls for untreated, fresh milk which is used within two hours of milking. It is easy to imagine the difficulties of transporting the milk on mules from the high grazing grounds to the cheese factory. Here the unskimmed milk is allowed to coagulate in the heaters using age-old procedures. There is no question of pasteurization: the perfect goodness and wholesomeness of the milk goes right into the cheese along with all its natural aroma. The batch obtained is placed in large

Suggested wines

- *Valle d'Aosta Chambave Rosso*
- *Pinot Nero Vigneto Consola -*
  Castello della Sala
- *Quattro Mori - Castel de' Paolis*
- *Cannonau di Sardegna*

Milk, eggs, butter, Fontina: a fondue is a high calorie dish perfect for the middle of winter.

round cheese molds that are left to rest a few hours before being moved to a cooler location. At this point the cheeses are salted and matured. The cheeses are placed on pine shelves. Every day they undergo delicate manual salting and cleaning of the surfaces with a brush dampened in a saline solution.

The maturing phase is very delicate and the producers have found a series of special "warehouses" (caves, military bunkers and even the abandoned copper mine of Ollomont). Temperature and humidity here are perfect for aging the cheese.

After about five months, the Fontina is ready in its cylindrical molds, about 7-8 cm in height and weighing between 8 and 18 kilos. The rind is thin, with a color that ranges from sienna to dark brown. On the rind is the label with the outline of the Matterhorn which indentifies the guardian consortium (practically speaking, the territorial limits for the origin of this cheese coincide with the regional borders). Inside it is a semisoft, elastic cheese with a color ranging

Recipe

FONDUE

Ingredients:
400 g / 1 pound Valle d'Aosta Fontina
50 g / 1,5 ounces butter
20 cl / 0,8 cup whole milk
3-4 egg yolks
salt and pepper to taste

Fondue is a bête noire for many cooks because it tends to curdle if the correct procedures are not followed. To ensure success, the first step is to soak the Fontina in the milk for at least three hours. At this point, the best method is to use a hemispherical bowl and cook the mixture in a bain-marie. Start by melting the butter and gradually add the Fontina with 3 or 4 tablespoons of the milk used for soaking. Using a whisk and moving continuously in the same direction, beat energetically until the mixture begins to go stringy. At this point, whisk in the egg yolks (only one at a time, without any interruption - so they need to be ready - and thoroughly blending in the first yolk before adding the next). At the end, the cheese mixture will lose its stringiness and have a nice creamy consistency. Add salt and white pepper and the fondue is ready. It can be served on its own, enriched with a sprinkling of truffles, or served with rice or polenta.

Fontina cheeses weigh between 8 and 18 kilos (photo: a typical maturing cellar).

from straw yellow to deeper shades typical of summer production. The taste is delicate and mild without any tendency towards being strong. According to some experts, Fontina can be eaten after three years of maturing, the end point of the maturing process, but its nobility is better expressed when young.

The "real" Valle d'Aosta Fontina bears a special label.

Residents of Valle d'Aosta are of the same opinion. In the middle of summer they hold cheese festivals at Etroubles and Oyace dedicated to this extraordinary component of Valle d'Aosta cuisine.
Fontina is a cheese with a very high fat content (about 45%) and it is rich in protein and calcium, making it a very nutritious food.
In cooking, the fact that it melts at 60°, means that it is used in a number of dishes, from the classic fondue to Valle d'Aosta polenta.

VALLE D'AOSTA FROMADZO

A must for tourists in Valle d'Aosta is a tour of the castles, all of them of an austere, medieval beauty. Near Verrès, going up to Issogne, there is also the opulent residence of the Challant, who built their palace towards the end of the 15th century, during the artistic transition from the Gothic to the more agile forms of the Renaissance. The imagination is struck by the harmonious courtyard with the stone fountain from which a wrought iron pomegranate rises, and by the precious frescoes decorating the reception rooms. Right here, in a vivacious scene from daily life, among the wares shown in a cheese shop, along with the traditional Fontina, is a cheese very much like today's Fromadzo, another jewel of Valle d'Aosta production. The local dialect has contained references to *fromage commun* or *fromadzo* (in Patois) since ancient times. The term "low fat" is often associated with the name, underlining its difference from the distinguished Fontina, with which it shares the same area of production, within the borders of Valle d'Aosta.
The production process calls for an almost exclusive use of cows' milk, with the possible addition of small quantities of

ewes' or goats' milk. Should a medium fat cheese be desired (with a fat content of between 20% and 35%), the milk is left to set for between 12 and 24 hours before skimming, while for a low fat cheese (containing not more than 20%) the time is extended to 24-36 hours. After coagulation, obtained with the addition of rennet, the temperature is brought up to 45°C. At this point the mixture is placed in molds (known as *feitchie* in dialect) and pressed lightly. Two equally important phases follow: the cheeses are turned over 3 or 4 times a day and salted (a very delicate process). After 20-30 days of this treatment, the rounds – 15-30 cm in diameter, between 5 and 20 cm high and weighing between 1 and 7 kilos – are put aside for maturing in locations where temperature and humidity are carefully controlled for a minimum of two and a maximum of ten months.
When served, fresh Fromadzo has a pale yellow rind and the interior is a lovely white color dotted with tiny eyes. The maturer cheeses have a deeper yellow rind and a straw yellow interior, which grows more intense in color the more the cheese is aged. It has a mild taste, with an elegant

Suggested wines

• *Vallée d'Aoste Blanc de Morgex et de la Salle*

• *Valtellina Sforzato*
• *Rosso Conero*
• *Vigna l'Apparita Merlot - Castello di Ama*

The quality of Fromadzo is due to the milk selected from the best pastures of the high mountains.

herbaceous aftertaste. The taste gets stronger with age, and ranges from slightly salty to strong. The fresh cheese, often with added aromas, is an excellent table cheese, while the aged, strong version can also be grated and is an excellent accompaniment for a classic risotto.

BRA

Bra has a singular charm with its fascinating Piazza Caduti per la Libertà, dominated by the baroque church of Sant'Andrea, whose opulent interior is by some attributed to Gian Lorenzo Bernini. With just a little more time, one can go on to Pollenzo, the Roman town Pollentia where Alaric and his Goths were defeated in 402. Today it is the site of the magnificent Royal Estate built in the 19th century by Carlo Alberto from a restructured 14th-century castle. But in Bra, the cheese of the same name is only found in specialized shops, because this gastronomic delicacy actually comes from somewhere else: from the plains of Cuneo and the towns in the valley below.

Our story starts with the herdsmen, or *bergé* as they are called in local dialect. With the first frosts of autumn, they descend to the plains with their herds from the Stura, Pesio, Po, Chisone, Pellice, Gesso, Grana and Varaita valleys. The specific cheese-making technique for what was once simply called *nostrale*, the local cheese, spread rapidly. The town of Bra (after which it was named) with its shrewd merchants, became the largest distribution center in Piedmont and the nearby

regions. It was particularly successful in Liguria where, especially in the last century, Parmesan cheese was used only to make the famous pesto for the rich man's table, while the common folk preferred aged cheese with a more decisive flavor and, not of lesser importance, a lower cost. Today Bra is produced throughout the province of Cuneo with a "summer pasture" variety produced by the mountain communes. It is made almost entirely of cows' milk, with the possible addition of tiny amounts of ewes' and/or goats' milk. Two types of Bra are produced: hard and soft. The first is pasteurized and heated to 35°C with the addition of rennet, and salted in brine, after which it is ripened for a month and a half. The second is processed at a lower temperature in huge heated copper vats, dry salted and left to mature for 6-12 months. The rounds are cylindrical, approximately 30-40 cm in diameter, between 7 and 9 cm high, and weighing no more than 8 kilos. Needless to say, there is a marked difference in taste between the hard and soft varieties. In the first case the rind is gray and rubbery and the cheese is somewhere between white and

Suggested wines

Soft cheese
- RIVIERA LIGURE DI PONENTE PIGATO

Soft cheese
- BARBERA D'ALBA
- DOLCETTO DI DOGLIANI

Hard cheese
- NEBBIOLO
- SALICE SALENTINO
- SAGRANTINO DI MONTEFALCO

ivory with a full, hearty taste, while the aged cheese is deep ochre with a more complex, austere taste and a sharp tang. In the kitchen Bra is an excellent grating cheese that can be a valid substitute for Grana (try it in pesto, after the old recipe from Liguria). The fresh type, cut into strips and dipped in egg and flour, is very tasty fried in butter, but it can also be melted over polenta or simply on toast.

Fat content is around 32%.

In Liguria, hard Bra is often used as a grating cheese when making a tasty pesto.

CASTELMAGNO

It is worth ascending to over 1000 meters, among the scattered houses and pastures of Castelmagno, the "capital" of one of Italy's noblest cheeses. Climbing even higher you come to the impressive sanctuary dedicated to a Roman legionnaire, who was martyred and subsequently beatified with the name of San Magno, where there are some interesting frescoes to admire. There is also a curious ancient epigraph dedicated to the cult of Mars, the pagan protector of weapons before that task was handed over to San Magno. Returning to our cheese, what is certain is that its name appeared in 1277 in a dispute among the valley's communes. The argument is proof that Castelmagno was already a precious ware in the medieval economy (at the time, a cheese was "traded" for twelve denarii). And in 1722, a decree signed by King Vittorio Amedeo II of Savoy granted the vassal of Castelmagno an "income of sixty-six lire and ten soldi per year, along with nine rubbi of cheese" (all to be paid by the local town, of course). During the last century, this cheese achieved a certain amount of prestige in international cuisine. Then, as the valley was abandoned (after

French experts consider Castelmagno one of Italy's most "aristocratic" cheeses.

World War II especially), it was almost lost from sight. In recent years, however, its reputation has been revived thanks to passionate interest from gastronomes and experts who have promoted the cheese both nationally and internationally. Now it is an irreplaceable item on the cheese-boards of "three star" restaurants the world over. The cheese is produced in the towns of Castelmagno,

Suggested wines

- *Barbaresco Sorì San Lorenzo - A. Gaja*
- *Amarone della Valpolicella*
- *Sassicaia - Tenuta San Guido Marchesi Incisa della Rocchetta*

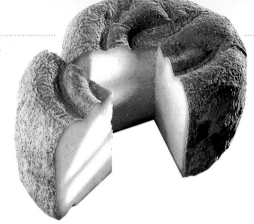

Recipe

GNOCCHI WITH CASTELMAGNO

Ingredients:
200 g / 7 ounces bleached flour
200 g / 7 ounces buck wheat flour
400 g / 1 pound cream
250 g / ½ pound slightly aged Castelmagno
salt and pepper to taste

Add water and a little salt to the flour and knead into dough. Then cover with a cloth and leave the dough to rest for an hour. Form the dough into small dumplings. Cut the Castelmagno into very small pieces, add to the cream and heat the mixture over a bain-marie. Mix well with a whisk. When the mixture forms a good, smooth cream, pour it over the gnocchi (small dumplings), which have already been cooked al dente in a large pan of salted water.

Pradleves and Monterosso Grana, all in the province of Cuneo. The basic ingredient is cows' milk with the optional addition of tiny amounts of ewes' and/or goats' milk. Two milkings are required to make the cheese, the first of which is left to rest overnight in a cool location (in the past, the pail was - and still is on occasion - immersed in the cold mountain streams). The batches are left to coagulate, forming large, uniform curds the size of walnuts. These are then placed in a *risolo*, a length of clean cloth hanging by a nail on a wall of the *malga*, a temporary wood and stone hut built in the Alpine summer pastures. This allows the whey to curdle properly in about twenty hours. After being broken up again into larger cubes, the curd from the various cloths is left to rest in a large wooden tub for another two days. The curd is then mixed using a sort of rudimentary mincer, and salted before being left to rest

again in a cheese mold for no more than three days. The cheese is pressed manually and then again with a mechanical press (in the past, large stones, called *lose*, were used to eliminate the whey), before being placed in cellars to ripen. These cellars, or *crote*, have tiny windows that let in little light and keep the atmosphere cool and dry. According to purists, the best *crote* have earthen floors and windows facing Monte Parvo, which rises 2500 meters above the sanctuary of San Magno. The maturing process lasts from two to five months. At that point the Castelmagno, with its typically elongated cylindrical form (between 15 and 20 cm in diameter, 12 and 20 cm in height, and weighing between 2 and 7 kilos) is ready.

The rind is reddish yellow and slightly rough in the more mature cheeses, while the interior is fairly crumbly and varies according to age from ivory to yellow with blue veins. The taste develops from being aristocratic, harmonious and salty to being heartier and stronger in flavor.

With a fat content of around 34%, Castelmagno can be eaten as a highly nutritional table cheese, or used in more elaborate dishes such as risotto or gnocchi.

GORGONZOLA

Recipe

SMALL GORGONZOLA SOUFFLÉ

Ingredients:
150 g / 5 ounces mild Gorgonzola
50 cl / 2 cups milk
80 g / 3 ounces flour
80 g / 3 ounces butter
4 eggs
salt and pepper to taste

Make a classic béchamel using the butter, milk and flour, blending in the Gorgonzola cut into fine strips, along with the four egg yolks. In another bowl beat the egg whites until stiff and blend into the béchamel, adding salt and pepper. Grease a shallow soufflé mold, fill it two thirds to the top and put into an oven preheated to 180°C. Cooking time is approximately half an hour.

There are numerous legends about the origin of Gorgonzola but they all agree that this great cheese, one of the most famous cheeses and the most frequently exported abroad, was born quite. According to some, an innkeeper in Gorgonzola, in Lombardy, found some locally produced *stracchino* streaked with mold (giving rise to the Italian term *erborinato*, since *erborin* means "parsley" in the local dialect and the moldy cheese looks as if it has been sprinkled with parsley). Not wanting to throw it away, he served it all the same. His guests were delighted with the new cheese which had a decisive taste that went so well with wine. And that was how, in the Middle Ages, *stracchino di Gorgonzola*, also known as *stracchino verde* (green stracchino) was born. According to another story, a cheese-maker absent-mindedly left his curd out overnight. The next day, so as not to waste it, he decided to "cut" it with the morning's milking, thus obtaining a cheese streaked with mold, similar to today's Gorgonzola. The link with this area of Lombardy is not altogether accidental given that the herds had to pass through the Po Valley on their return from the summer pastures. Others insist that Gorgonzola originated in Novara, recollecting the large natural cellars of the Valsassina, *casere*, which have been the ideal location for this cheese to age since ancient times.

Today the area of production of real Gorgonzola is quite large, and includes two regions, Piedmont and Lombardy, comprising the provinces of Cuneo, Alessandria, Vercelli, Novara, Milan, Pavia, Cremona, Bergamo, Brescia, and Como. Actually, it was in the province of Como, in Bellagio Inferiore, that Mattia Locatelli built the first factory for high quality industrial production in the second half of the 19th century.

Two distinct types of Gorgonzola can be found today: the so-called *a due paste*, which is much older and has the rich, strong flavor so loved by connoisseurs, and another that is much milder (it is also more common, both because processing is simpler and because it is preferred by consumers), *una pasta*.

For the *due paste* type, the evening's milking is used. This is filtered (but not skimmed) and coagulated. Once it has been cut down to pieces the size of hazelnuts, the curd is gathered in canvas cloths known as *patte* and placed on

The creamy, sharp taste of Gorgonzola makes it a perfect accompaniment for vegetables and canapés as an appetizer.

wooden trestles overnight for the whey to drain away. In this way, it is naturally exposed to the specific spores which create the mold. This mixture, called the "cold curd" is combined with the hot curd from the next morning's milking which has been left to coagulate for less than an hour. At this point in the process, the cheese molds are filled with alternating layers of the hot and cold curds (up to eleven layers can be added). The molds are placed on an inclined plane, called a

spersola, so that the cheese can start to dry, after which it is moved to a storage room, or *purgatorio,* where the temperature is kept at a constant 22°C and the humidity is very high.

A few days later, the cheese-maker starts salting the cheese, rubbing it on both sides with a mixture containing a little carotene (clay was used in the past) which makes the rind firm and gives it a pleasant reddish color. Salting lasts about 20 days. Immediately after that, the actual maturing process starts, split into two phases: drying and maturing.

The first phase lasts from three to four weeks at a temperature of about 20°C and relative humidity of about 80%. The cheeses are covered with a light, reddish mold, the sign of correct maturing (the appearance of a black mold means that the cheeses have to be thrown away). After maturing, the cheeses are pierced on all sides with long metal skewers, (copper or steel), in place of the seasoned wood used in the past. This procedure lets the air circulate inside the cheese so that the mold is evenly distributed. The main difference in the processing of *una pasta* Gorgonzola lies in the fact that whole milk from a single milking is used. It is coagulated in a vat at 30°C incorporating milk enzymes, rennet and penicillus spores (which cause the mold). The curds are then broken up and placed in small cheese molds for the whey to drain and away to the *purgatorio* for salting. During this processing, after three or four weeks curing, these cheeses are also pierced. They are then allowed to rest again before being marketed, wrapped in their distinctive, thin aluminium foil which is designed to protect the special characteristics of this cheese. The cheeses are cylindrical, about 16-20 cm high, 25-30 cm

in diameter, and weighing between 6 and 13 kilos in total. From a gastronomic point of view, Gorgonzola is a wonderful table cheese, with a creamy, sharp taste and a fat content of 48%.

According to taste, one may enjoy the mild version, with its very creamy interior and a hint of mold, or the stronger variety, with its more crumbly interior and distinctive mold.

There are a number of green-veined cheeses in the world, especially in France, which are reminiscent of the taste of Gorgonzola: *Roquefort, Bleu de Bresse, Fourme d'Ambert* as well as the English *Stilton*. However, the richness and complexity of Italy's Gorgonzola are unrivalled. It is no accident that this cheese lends itself to a huge number of culinary variations. It is delicious as an accompaniment to raw vegetables (celery, fennel), on canapés or in a risotto.

Suggested wines

- *Marsala Vergine*
- *Chambave Moscato Passito Picolit*

- *Amarone della Valpolicella*

MURAZZANO

Gastronomes look upon the Langhe as a region of unbridled happiness, the home of some of Italy's greatest wines as well as the precious white truffle, which is irreplaceable in the preparation of Piedmont's best dishes. The area is a group of enchanting hills dotted with vineyards, in a landscape of great peace where forbidding castles and medieval hamlets testify to the fact that man has been here for a long time. This is where Murazzano is born, a soft, fat, fresh cheese, part of the great Robiola family. The term *Robiola* is apparently derived from the Latin *rubeola* (from *rubens*) because of the reddish color of the rind. There are, however, also those who believe that the name can be traced back to the commune of Robbio, in Lombardy's Lomellina. It is no accident that Piedmont and Lombardy both claim to be the birthplace of this cheese, which is also mentioned in a quote by the learned Pliny who praised the goodness of the cheese of Ceva, made primarily with ewes' milk.

There is still a type of Murazzano made entirely of ewes' milk (although the law allows the addition of up to 40% cows' milk) in a vast area that includes many communities

Suggested wines

- DOLCETTO D'ALBA
- TEROLDEGO ROTALIANO
- SANGIOVESE DI ROMAGNA

The delicate taste of Murazzano makes it perfect for a delicious cream cheese with herbs.

Recipe

MURAZZANO CREAM CHEESE

Ingredients
500 g / 1 pound Murazzano
3 cloves of garlic
1 laurel leaf
1 bouquet garni (tarragon, chives, thyme, marjoram, sweet basil, summer savory)

The procedure is very simple. Chop the herbs very finely before incorporating them into the cheese with a blender (a drop of oil may be added to facilitate blending). When the Murazzano cream cheese is ready, it should be placed in small terracotta jars, sealed tightly and kept refrigerated. Delicious on pieces of hot toast.

in Alta Langa and the province of Cuneo. The milk is coagulated at 37°C and the curd is placed in special tiny cheese molds with holes in the bottom to let the whey drain off. Curing lasts no more than 10 days, after which the cheese is sold. The cheeses are 10-15 cm in diameter and are about 3 cm high. They have no rind and the cheese is a lovely white which tends to turn pale yellow as it matures. It has a refined, delicate taste with a pleasant, slightly herbaceous aftertaste that reminds one of the milk of the region's sheep which graze during the summer and have high quality hay as their winter fodder.

With a fat content of 53%, Murazzano (named only recently after one of the communities of Alta Langa where it is produced), is a typical table cheese to be eaten on its own or with a small quantity of extra-virgin olive oil and salt and pepper.

RASCHERA

Suggested wines

Young cheese
• VERNACCIA DI SAN GIMIGNANO

Youngcheese
• DOLCETTO DI DOGLIANI
• ROSSO OLTREPÒ PAVESE
Mature cheese
• BARBARESCO
• ORNELLAIA - TENUTA DELL'ORNELLAIA

On Ferragosto, the 15th of August and the Feast of the Assumption, at Frabosa Soprana, in the Mondovì valley in the province of Cuneo, there is a huge Raschera cheese fair. It is a perfect occasion to discover this delicious cheese from the Cuneo area, with the label *di alpeggio* (from summer pastures) when produced in localities above 900 meters. It is also an opportunity to visit the lovely cave of Bossea with its splendid rock formations, waterfalls and pools.

Raschera seems to have taken its name from the lake on the slopes of Monte Mongioie, although some say it is named after the nearby Rascaira Alps. Raschera is a half-fat cheese made of cows' milk, with the possible addition of ewes' or goats' milk. Processing is fairly complex. Two daily milkings are used and are coagulated at between 27°C and 30°C in a typical wooden vat, called a *gerla*, which is covered with a woolen cloth. The curd is cut and then beaten to obtain a mass which is separated from the whey. It is then wrapped in a canvas cloth and placed in the cheese mold. Here it is pressed a little, the mass is again cut into pieces and undergoes pressing for 24 hours.

The cheeses (which are either round or square) are hand-rubbed with salt and pierced to allow for even distribution. After maturing, which lasts from twenty days to three months (giving the cheese a more decisive, stronger taste), the Raschera is ready for sale. The cylindrical cheeses are 35-40 cm in diameter, 7-9 cm high and have a fat content of about 32%. The square cheeses, on the other hand, have a sharper flavor because they are pressed longer. They are about 40 cm on each side, about 15 cm high and weigh about 10 kilos. The story goes that this type of Raschera is the result of a storage mishap (the rounds were stored one on top of another in the summer huts in the Alps and the ones on the bottom came out misshapen). Be that as it may, in the past the square type was certainly much simpler to handle (and therefore much more popular) during the trip by mule to the markets of Liguria (with its insatiable desire for cheese).

The cheese is a fine ivory color with small, irregular eyes and a delicate, aromatic taste that becomes decidedly stronger as the cheese ages. Raschera is an excellent table cheese and can also be eaten as an accompaniment to polenta or a plate of gnocchi.

Only the Raschera produced in the towns over 900 meters in the province of Cuneo is priveleged to have the "di alpeggio" label (from summer pastures).

ROBIOLA DI ROCCAVERANO

- *GAVI DI GAVI*
- *VERDICCHIO DI MATELICA*
- *VERMENTINO DI GALLURA*

- *BARBERA D'ASTI*

Roccaverano is a place of great charm, dominated by the ruins of a castle and the Church of the Assumption with its elegant Renaissance forms reminiscent of Bramante. Gastronomes can visit the town in September during the fair dedicated to its famous Robiola, a fresh cheese made with a maximum of 85% cows' milk and the addition of ewes' or goats' milk (which is the only ingredient in the ultra-traditional Robiola so dear to gourmets, not least because of its capacity to

Connoisseurs who love traditional foods are particularly fond of the Robiola made only with goat's milk.

Grappa, black pepper and hot red pepper: bruss is really an "explosive mixture".

withstand aging). Be that as it may, the quality of the milk depends on the herds' special green fodder, which is enriched with the bramble, aromatic herbs and thyme scattered over the slopes of these mountains. Liquid rennet is then added to the milk at a temperature of 18°C and the milk is left to rest for a day in the molds. At this point, after light salting, the cheese is left to rest for another 72 hours or else left to mature for two or three weeks (this applies especially to the goats' milk variety). Robiola is commonly preserved in olive oil with the addition of herbs. The cheeses are cylindrical and weigh between 200 and 400 grams. There is no rind and the flavor is delicate with a slightly acid aftertaste. Robiola of Roccaverano (the protected area of production is situated between the provinces of Asti and Alessandria) is an excellent table cheese. It is also delicious preserved in olive oil or eaten with the classic *bagnet*, a traditional sauce of parsley, garlic, bread, and a little anchovy.

Recipe

BRUSS

"L'amor l'è pi fort che'l bruss", love is stronger than bruss, according to the old Piedmontese adage. Actually, with its strong taste, the first impact of this cheese dish can be quite violent indeed. Bruss is made using whole Robiola cheeses (although it was originally made of leftovers so that nothing was thrown away), placed in an earthenware pot with half a glass of grappa and a healthy dose of ground black pepper and hot red pepper. The mixture is covered with extra-virgin olive oil and left to rest for a few days. It is then stirred with a wooden spoon and left in a cool place until fermentation begins. At that point the pot is moved to a warmer area and covered with a plate with a weight on top. It takes bruss about a month to ripen, after which it is eaten spread on bread, to make the most of all its pungent flavor.

TOMA PIEMONTESE

Suggested wines

- *Isonzo Vieris Sauvignon - Vie di Romans*
- *Collio Chardonnay - Gravner*

- *Lagrein*

In Piedmont, the word *toma* is almost synonymous with the word cheese. The etymology is uncertain, however, and seems to be derived from the Franco-Provençal *tumer*, meaning "fall", in reference to the precipitation of the milk protein under the effect of the rennet. In any event, the origins of this cheese go back a long way; it is so old that it is mentioned in a learned treatise, *Summa lacticiniorum*, published in Turin in 1477 by court physician Pantaleone da Confienza. Here Toma is called *caseus mordicativus*, referring to its pungent, strong taste.

Today, Toma is produced throughout Piedmont, from areas in the provinces of Turin, Biella, Novara, and Vercelli to numerous towns around Alessandria and Asti. Only cows' milk is used, either whole (making a softer, creamier cheese) or partly skimmed. Generally two consecutive milkings are used. After the milk is heated in a vat, rennet is added.

The batch is left to rest and then heated again to a higher temperature until the curd sinks to the bottom, completely

In Piedmont, Toma is the epitome of cheese.

Rye bread and Toma: a simple soup with an old-fashioned taste.

separated from the whey. It is then placed in the mold and left to ripen for a day. In the meantime, the cheeses are turned over again and again and hand-rubbed with salt. Maturing takes place in cellars or cool areas with a relative humidity of about 85%. After a period of fifteen days to two months, depending on the weight of the cheeses, the Toma is ready. It has a smooth, straw-colored rind. The cheese is light in color, with only a few eyes.

The mild, harmonious taste becomes pungent after prolonged aging.
The cheeses are cylindrical, between 15 and 35 cm in diameter, 6 to 12 cm in height, and weighing between 2 and 8 kilos. They have a fat contant at least 18%.
Toma is an excellent table cheese but it also lends itself to cooking where, for example, it is used in the well-known *polenta concia* and in some soups.

BITTO

Recipe

SCIATT

Ingredients:
300 g / 8 ounces buckwheat flour
300 g / 8 ounces bleached flour
300 g / 8 ounces fairly young
Bitto
1 glass good grappa
lard
salt to taste

*Make a fairly thick batter, mixing
the two kinds of sifted flour,
slightly salted, with a little
lukewarm water. Cover with a
cloth and allow to rest at room
temperature. Cut the Bitto into
fine strips and blend into the
batter, adding the grappa. Melt
the lard in a pan and fry the
fritters (poured from a spoon).
Keep the temperature high,
otherwise the cheese will not melt
like Mozzarella and the fritters
will absorb too much lard,
making them heavy.*

The Valtellina is one of the most beautiful mountain areas in the Alps. Bormio, a hamlet of tiny alleyways lined with ancient buildings with their heavy, decorated front doors, especially deserves a visit. Here, there is also the Collegiata, renovated during baroque times, where the *kuerc,* the pavilion where justice was administered, is still standing.

Bitto, of truly ancient origin and one of Italy's most renowned cheeses, was born amidst these mountain-dominated landscapes. Apparently it was the Celts, pushed back north of the Po Valley by the Romans, who taught the local populations with whom they mixed the art of cheese-making. It is no accident that the word Bitto - also the name of the river flowing from the Gerola and Albaredo valleys into the Adda - seems to have come from the Celtic *bitu,* meaning "eternal", presumably in reference to the cheese's capacity for lasting a long time in comparison to the fresh curds traditionally found on Roman tables.

Undoubtedly due to the isolation so typical of the Valtellina area, almost nothing has changed in the production of Bitto from those far-off centuries to our times. Interestingly enough, in medieval times, Bitto was used by the locals as a trading currency.

Today the production area covers the province of Sondrio as well as some towns in the territory of Bergamo. The cheese is made almost entirely of cows' milk, with the addition of a little goats' milk, which gives it its special consistency and distinctive taste.

It is made during the summer, during the standard 84 days of summer pasture. Artisan techniques are used and production is entrusted to the "loaders", as the men in charge of the cows are called. The fresh milk is taken to the *calécc,* the summer Alpine huts with stone walls, and left to coagulate at a temperature of between 39°C and 49°C, assisted by the microflora that appears. The cheese is then placed in molds and regularly salted by hand for at least three weeks. The cheeses, 30 to 50 cm wide, 8 to 10 cm high, weighing between 8 and 25 kilos, and having a fat content of 45%, are taken to dairies down in the valley to mature for a minimum of three months. After three years, Bitto is thought to have reached its peak but the cheeses can easily

Sciatt, flavored with grappa, is a mouth-watering cheese fritter.

be left to age for up to ten years, developing a more complex, refined taste, much appreciated by gourmets. The young cheese is soft and whitish with a mild taste and a pleasant, aromatic aftertaste. As it ages, the taste becomes stronger and the cheese becomes firm and crumbly like Grana, even though it keeps a touch of the creaminess that is one of its characteristics.

Due to fairly limited production, Bitto is very rare. It is excellent as a table cheese and in a number of dishes, including a sauce for the traditional *pizzoccheri*, wide wheat/buckwheat flour noodles, and *polenta taragna* made with buckwheat flour, *fraina*.

Suggested wines

- *Valtellina Sfursat*
- *Vino nobile di Montepulciano*
- *Aglianico del Vulture*

FORMAI DE MUT DELL'ALTA VAL BREMBANA

Suggested wines

- *FRANCIACORTA ROSSO*
- *PINOT NERO VIGNETO S. URBANO -*
  HOFSTÄTTER

- *CHARDONNAY -*
TASCA D'ALMERITA REGALEALI

Foppolo, Branzi, Carona, all popular winter ski resorts, are just a few of the mountain communes in the Bergamo area. And the mountains must also be mentioned in relation to the pride of the cheese-making tradition of the Alta Val Brembana: Formai de Mut (cheese of the mount), a jewel produced according to an age-old, unchanging process.

It is made from the milk of the brown Alpine cow (there are 17th century documents regarding imports of Swiss and German cattle to improve local breeds which testify to the locals' love for their work). The cows are fed on grass and fodder in pastures at altitudes of 1200 to 2500 meters. The herdsmen work in *casere* (their devout practise of supplying the cellars with a small image of Sant'Antonio Abate, the patron saint of cattle, is eloquent), stone mountain huts, which are often underground, and oriented to avoid much of the sun's light in order to ensure a constant temperature of between 9°C and 13°C. This is the temperature required for the chemical enzyme reactions, essential for the excellent flavor of this cheese, to take place. The fresh milk (10 liters are needed to make 1 kilo of Formai de Mut) is poured into enormous, 400 liter vats where it is curdled. The mass is extracted with *pate*, large canvases which also allow for draining, and placed in circular molds.

The dry cheese is salted every other day for a little over two weeks. The minimum ripening time is a month and a half for table cheese and up to two months for the stronger cheese. The cheeses are cylindrical, 30 to 40 cm in diameter, between 8 and 10 cm in height, and weighing about 10 kilos. The rind is firm and thin, and light yellow or gray depending on the age.

The cheese is a lovely ivory color, sprinkled with small eyes and with a delicate, mellow taste, reminiscent of Alpine milk.

Formai de Mut is also delectable melted over cornmeal *polenta*, the traditional poor man's dish in these hills.

BAGÓSS

Bagolino is a cheerful village in the Valle del Caffaro in the province of Brescia. This is where Bagóss is produced, the name coming from a word in dialect meaning "from Bagolino".

The cheese is made of untreated cows' milk following artisan procedures. It was introduced to the gourmet public thanks to the enthusiasm of Chef Benedetto Girelli di Barghe who also distributed a book full of appetizing recipes.

The cheese is made by *malgari*, or herdsmen, and requires laborious procedures. It suffices to say that salting is carried out by hand for no less than three months and that each cheese is carefully brushed and turned over to keep mildew from forming. When they are finally ready, the cylindrical cheeses measure 40 cm in diameter and about 14 cm in height, and weigh about 15 kilos. The rind, rubbed with raw linseed oil to keep it elastic, is brown, while the cheese is pale straw yellow. Bagóss has a full, rich, aromatic taste. It can be eaten as a table cheese but it is also perfect for grating, especially in its mature form.

Suggested wines

- FRANCIACORTA ROSSO
- GRANATO - FORADORI
- MARCHESE DI VILLAMARINA - SELLA & MOSCA

Recipe

PENNE WITH BAGÓSS

Ingredients:
350 g / 12 ounces penne
200 g / 7 ounces Bagóss
4 rashers of fat bacon
salt and pepper to taste.

This recipe is very easy. Boil the penne pasta "al dente" and season with a knob of butter, the grated Bagóss and a tablespoonful of the cooking water. Add salt and pepper to taste and grill briefly in the oven with a rasher of bacon laid on each individual plate.

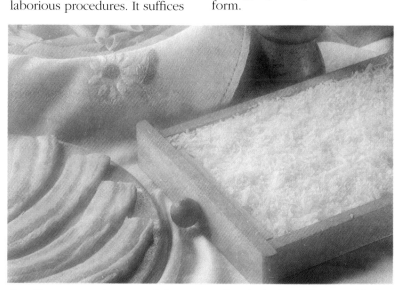

Excellent on penne, a type of short pasta, Bagóss is also delicious grilled.

PROVOLONE VALPADANA

Today, Provolone is a typical product of the Po Valley region, but it most certainly originated as one of the typical stringy cheeses of Southern Italy, such as Provola, Scamorza or Caciocavallo. According to experts, it was first produced near Potenza in the South. The first documented references to this cheese are found in Canevazzi's *Vocabolario di Agricoltura* in 1871 and the creation of the Margiotti brothers' cheese-making factory in the lower Brescia areas, again during the second half of the 19th century. Originally from Montelucano, the brothers had moved north where the abundance of milk allowed them to more easily practice the art of cheese-making. Provolone's main characteristic is that it is spun, an essential technique which gives it its special structure and flavor.

Processing starts with pure cows' milk, to which milk enzymes with a high acidifying power are added. The milk is then coagulated with liquid calf rennet for the mild type (which is also briefly aged) or kid rennet paste, the so-called "strong rennet", for the strong type (which is aged for a longer period of time). The curd is kneaded like dough until it becomes stringy and rubbery. The cheese-maker then shapes the cheeses, as though they were clay, taking care that the surfaces are smooth and that no air bubbles or liquid residues are left inside. The cheese is closed at the top and left in cold water to harden. Salting takes place in brine (a saturated solution of water and salt), and the cheeses are hung to ferment in warm rooms (trade regulations also allow smoking of the cheeses here) and matured for a minimum of a month for the mild cheese and for periods of over six months for the strong cheese.

Given the ease with which they can be modelled, the cheeses can have different shapes, from the classic "truncated cone", to the "salami", the "tangerine" and the "belly-shaped", all familiar names used by consumers. Weight also varies a great deal, from cheeses of half a kilo for home consumption, to a hundred kilos. The cheese is a lovely straw yellow color and the

rind is smooth with indentations made by the cords used to hang them during aging.

The area of production includes the provinces of Trento, Verona, Vicenza, Rovigo, Padua, Piacenza, Milan, Bergamo, Brescia, Mantua and Cremona (historically the "capital" of this cheese). The taste ranges from mild and buttery to strong, according to the type and age. Apart from the fact that Provolone is a highly nutritious cheese, its capacity to become thready and melt make it a very versatile ingredient in cooking. But don't forget that Provolone is also delicious just as a table cheese.

Provolone comes in various shapes: the classic truncated cone, but also shaped like a "salami", "tangerine" or "belly".

QUARTIROLO

In Lombardy, the stubby grass that grows after the third mowing in the summer is known as *erba quartirola*, the fourth mowing hay. The cattle were fed on this final crop before the cold months and their milk was used to produce a characteristic soft cheese, called Quartirolo. Times have changed and this cheese – which, like Taleggio, belongs to the large family of *stracchino* cheeses (so called because they come from the milk of cows that are *stracche*, weary, from the long journey from the summer pastures to the valley) – is produced all year long. The area of production includes the provinces of Milan, Cremona, Pavia, Bergamo, Brescia, Como, and Varese.

The cheese is made with coagulated skimmed or whole milk. In two successive phases, the curd is then broken into progressively smaller pieces. Immediately afterwards, it is placed in cheese molds and stored at a temperature of around 28°C for a 4 to 24 hour period of fermentation.

Curing no longer takes place in

Quartirolo is an elegant member of the Stracchino family.

Authentic Quartirolo can be recognized by its square shape, the distinctive label on top and its pinkish rind.

Suggested wines

- *FELDMARSHALL VON FENNER - TIEFENBRUNNER*
- *VERNACCIA DI SAN GIMIGNANO*

- *ROSSO OLTREPÒ PAVESE PINOT NERO*

caves, on wooden *scalere*, step-ladders, covered with straw. The cheeses are matured in special cells where temperature and humidity are kept constant for a period of between five days (for the softer type) to the thirty days needed for the typical Quartirolo Lombardo. The cheeses are quadrangular in shape, and are 20 cm long and about 5 cm high, weighing between 1 and 9 kilos. The rind is a pinkish white, with grayish hints in the more mature cheeses. The cheese is soft and whitish with a delicate taste which is slightly acid in the fresh cheese, while mature Quartirolo is more pungent.

It is a typical table cheese, perfect with a lovely green salad sprinkled with walnuts. Leftover cheese, blended with a little fresh Mascarpone and a few drops of cognac or gin, makes a delicious cream cheese to spread on warm canapés as a hors d'œuvre.

TALEGGIO

Giacomo Casanova, the great expert in aphrodisiacs (he was renowned for using oysters to seduce two young nuns), discovered Taleggio in 1762 while staying with the Attendolo Bolognini family at Sant'Angelo Lodigiano to write a book about cheese (never completed). But this cheese was already considered a choice delicacy fit for the guests at the nuptials of Bianca Maria Visconti and Francesco Sforza in 1441. The name Taleggio is fairly recent (in the past it was known as Stracchino di Taleggio), and results from the desire to distinguish this high quality product from the many similar cheeses produced in Lombardy and outlying areas. Today, the area of production includes Bergamo, Brescia, Como, Milan, Cremona, Pavia, Novara, and Treviso, but in the past production was concentrated in the Val Taleggio in the province of Bergamo (from whence its name).

This cheese is made from whole, heated cows' milk, to which a little of the previous day's whey (the *innesto,* or graft) and calf rennet are added. The curd is cut twice (the second time with a cup-shaped brass instrument with sharp edges called a *tas*). It is then placed in square molds of about 20 cm on each side and about 6 cm high. After fermenting for almost 18 hours in a storage area with a high

Suggested wines

- *Gavi di Gavi - La Scolca*
- *Verdicchio dei Castelli di Jesi*

- *Rosso Oltrepò Pavese Pinot Nero*

Taleggio was served as a costly delicacy at the wedding of Bianca Maria Visconti and Francesco Sforza in 1441.

Taleggio with dried tomatoes: a seductive recipe dating back to Casanova's time.

Recipe

FRESH TALEGGIO WITH DRIED TOMATOES

Ingredients:
300 g / 10 ounces fresh Taleggio
100 g / 3 ½ ounces dried tomatoes in olive oil
1 shallot
1 glass of red wine

Place slices of Taleggio on each plate. Sauté the chopped shallot in a little oil, add the tomatoes cut into thin strips and sauté, adding the red wine. Place the tomatoes on the Taleggio and garnish with herbs (for example marjoram, thyme, fresh oregano).

humidity, the Taleggio is cured in rooms with a low temperature and high humidity for about 25-30 days. Today, most of the cheese is cured in areas with modern temperature regulation equipment, but about a third of the production is taken up to the mountains for perfect maturing. In this phase, the rind is sponged down with brine once a week to prevent mildew, which would ruin the rind's from forming pinkish color. Taleggio has a fat content of about 48%. The cheese is soft and creamy and the rind is thin. It has a pungent aroma and a decisive taste with a pleasantly aromatic, creamy texture.
It is primarily a table cheese, but given the ease with which it melts, it is also eaten on polenta and served with a number of pasta dishes or on grilled vegetables.

VALTELLINA CASERA

Valtellina is a region where cattle-breeding plays a central role in the local economy. Even Leonardo da Vinci in his *Codice Atlantico* mentioned the area, reminiscing about the height of the mountains and the strength of the wines, where the only thing produced in larger quantities was milk.

Today, within the borders of the province of Sondrio, apart from the famous Bitto, the characteristic Casera cheese is produced. Casera is made of pure cows' milk which has been left to stand for half a day before being skimmed, in order to encourage the growth of the cheese microflora. The milk is coagulated in a vat at a temperature of 37°C with calf rennet. The curd is broken first into small pieces and heated again to a temperature of 42°C to 43°C before being transferred into cheese molds where the whey is drained away for about half a day. Dry salting is carried out using brine. Maturing – carried out in rooms with a high level of humidity – is never less than two months.

The cheeses are cylindrical, from 30 to 45 cm in diameter and about 10 cm in height. They weigh between 7 and 12 kilos and have a fat content of about 34%. The rind is straw yellow and the cheese varies in color from white to pale yellow with scattered eyes. The taste is mellow, mild and pleasantly fragrant.

Casera from Valtellina is an excellent table cheese, while the more mature variety can be grated to enrich a risotto.

Suggested wines

- VALTELLINA SFURSAT 5 STELLE - NEGRI
- REFOSCO PEDUNCOLO ROSSO
- VINO NOBILE DI MONTEPULCIANO

GRANA PADANO

- *AMARONE DELLA VALPOLICELLA*
- *BAROLO SPERS - A. GAJA*
- *MARCHESE DI VILLAMARINA - SELLA & MOSCA*

Grana Padano can boast a very ancient history indeed. It dates back to around the year 1000 when the Cistercian monks of Chiaravalle began to reclaim the marshy, wood-covered lands in lower Lombardy. The availability of farmland allowed for the development of cattle-raising and, therefore, for a greater production of milk. The need to keep the milk from going bad led to the development of the art of making cheese, and the production of cheese that could be aged for long periods in particular. This is how Grana, so called for its grainy interior, came to be, in the square area bordered by the Adda, the Mincio, the Po and Milan. It was immediately successful; so much so that in 1334, it appeared on the list of provisions of the Priors of Florence, was carried in galleys during long sea voyages because of its durability, and was cited as Italy's most famous cheese (with the name of *Piacentino*) in the treatise on cheeses written by Pantaleone da Confienza, physician to the House of Savoy, in 1477.

Centuries later, except for the understandable changes made to comply with health standards, Grana Padano is still produced according to ancient traditions. The procedure starts with the milk cows, which are fed on water and pure fodder, untouched by pesticides. The pure milk is partially skimmed and coagulated in copper vats holding 1000 liters (the amount needed to make two cheeses). The curd is broken into pieces, drained and again heated to about 55°C. At this point, the batch is divided in half and the two rubbery batches are salted in brine for about four weeks. Only then is the Grana left to mature, in special locations where the temperature is between 18°C and 20°C and the humidity is about 85%. The typical cylindrical cheeses are between 35 and 45 cm in diameter, between 18 and 25 cm high, and weigh between 25 and 40 kilos (the size is another characteristic of this cheese). At the beginning of the maturing process, the cheeses are branded with the figure of a four-leaf clover and an ID number. It is only after maturing, however (during which time the cheeses are constantly turned over and cleaned), that an exacting inspectorate examines the cheese. A hammer (to detect any empty spaces inside the cheese) and a drill (to taste) are used to see whether the cheese deserves the lozenge-shaped label of the consortium (stamped all over the cheese to

In the 18th century, snow was used to make this Grana Padano ice.

Recipe

GRANA PADANO ICE

Ingredients:
500 g / 1 pound Grana Padano
1 l / 4 cups cream
salt and pepper to taste

This dish is extremely old; at one time, snow was used to turn it into ice-cream. Grate the Grana Padano, mix with the cream and cook in a casserole over a bain-marie, adding salt and pepper. Once the mixture has become creamy, allow it to cool, pass through a sieve and place in an ice-cream maker and proceed according to the usual methods for making ice-cream.

avoid fraud on small pieces). The well-known exception is the cheese with the stronger aroma and taste produced in the province of Trento. It is stamped "Grana Trentino", on condition that it is produced with milk from Alpine cows and is made using a technique that combines mountain cheese-making traditions with the rigorous standards for this cheese.

Grana Padano has a crumbly interior that can be broken into flakes (a special almond-shaped knife should be used). Color ranges from white with a touch of pale yellow to more intense shades for mature cheeses. It has a distinctive aroma and an elegant, flavorsome taste. It is perfect for grating but can also be used as a table cheese with a variety of uses. It is a popular cheese for those who practice sport since it is highly digestible and rich in minerals and proteins. It was in fact an official food of Italy's national soccer team when it won the World Cup in Spain, the official cheese of the 1990 World Cup in Italy, and of the World Track and Field Federations.

Tasters hit the cheeses with a hammer. The proper "timbre" is the sign of a good product.

ASIAGO

From the town of Asiago one can see the huge Military Memorial Chapel dedicated to the Italian and Austro-Hungarian soldiers killed during World War I. The view of the upland plain with its seven famous towns among the wide plains, fields and silent evergreen forests evokes a feeling of peace. It is natural to suppose that sheep-grazing has been an important economic resource since antiquity. Originally, the traditional cheese in the area was made from sheeps'milk, and the old highlanders still call Asiago *pegurìn*, ewes' milk cheese. Over time, however, the move towards more profitable cattle-breeding influenced cheese production as well.

Authentic Asiago is produced in an area that includes the provinces of Vicenza and Trento and part of the provinces of Padua and Treviso. Today it is made from the milk of Frisian and brown Alpine

Frisian and brown Alpine cows provide the milk for the classic Asiago.

cows. Two varieties are produced. The more traditional cheese is known as *d'allevo*, meaning cultivated, a term used to indicate the care taken over maturing, and the result can be either *mezzana*, dependent upon a maturing period of three to five months, or *vecchia* when the cheese is matured for over nine months. Two milkings are coagulated together, the curd reduced to the size of grains of rice and then cooked. The batch is placed in the cheese mold and salted. There is also another type of Asiago which has become very popular with consumers because of its milder taste (the result of a shorter ripening period, from three to six weeks). The cheeses are cylindrical, between 30 and 36 cm in diameter, about 10 cm high, and weigh between 9 and 12 kilos, with a fat content of about 34%. The cheese is straw yellow and evenly dotted with eyes.

Asiago is an excellent table cheese, both the mild, delicate variety, and the *d'allevo* variety (which has a strong flavor, particularly in the case of the more mature cheeses), which also has many gastronomic uses and a high nutritional value. One hundred grams of Asiago contain 30.6 grams of protein, equivalent to 147 grams of veal, 160 grams of chicken and as much as 210 grams of fish.

MONTASIO

Recipe

FRICO

Ingredients:
250 g / ½ pound aged Montasio
100 g / 3 ½ ounces fresh Montasio
100 g / 3 ½ ounces butter
1 white onion
salt and pepper to taste

This dish is very popular throughout Friuli but it is also found in Veneto with the name of "schizz". This is one of the many versions: cut the onion into very fine pieces and sauté in butter. Before the onion is too golden, add the cheese, cut into small pieces, and salt (not too much, aged Montasio is already quite strong) and pepper. When the mixture is crisp and blended together, turn it over as if it were an omelette and finish cooking on the other side.

The town of Codroipo is not far from Villa Manin at Passariano. A festival is held here every October in honor of San Simone during which Montasio is at its peak. The cheese apparently dates back to a specific production method invented in the 13th century by a monk at the Abbey of Moggio which owned the *malghe* (temporary wood and stone huts in the summer pastures) of the Montasio Alps in Friuli. At the end of the 18th century, price-lists from San Daniele show that Montasio was renowned and was already worth a pretty penny. The real fortune of this cheese, however, came about a century later with the birth of the cooperative movement and collective dairies which played an important role in the Friuli economy. Production calls for the use of milk from the prized spotted red heifer. It also calls for non-pasteurization (or a "soft" technique at any rate) to preserve the product's excellent taste. The milk is coagulated and the batch of curd chopped into fragments the size of grains of rice with a special curd knife known as a *lira*. It is then cooked "fuori fuoco" (off the heat), a procedure that makes the curd harder. The curd is then removed with special cloths and placed in the molds. A pressing phase follows to drain off the whey, after which salting in brine takes place. According to the length of ripening the cheese can be "fresh" (sixty days), *mezzano* (average quality – between five and twelve months) and *stravecchio* (matured – over a year). The cheese thus ranges from white with regular eyes, a rubbery consistency and a mild taste, to yellow with a strong taste and crumbly consistency. From a gastronomic point of view, Montasio is an excellent table cheese, while the aged version is ideal for grating. There is another delicious version of Montasio which is not covered by trade regulations. This cheese, known as "drunken" Montasio, is aged in grape must. It is clearly a close relative of the *formaio embriago* (drunken cheese), made in Trevigiano. The cheese is immersed in must containing pieces of Cabernet or Merlot grapes and, after four or five days, reaches the same level of maturity as a cheese which has been aged for five or six months. The rind is a violet color but the must does not touch the interior, which is, however, quite aromatic. The grape must used is then thrown away, making the process quite costly.

MONTE VERONESE

Suggested wines

- VINTAGE TUNINA - VINNAIOLI JERMANN
- SOAVE CLASSICO

- SANGIOVESE DI ROMAGNA
- PINOT NERO VILLA BARTHENAU - HOFSTÄTTER

Verona, the city of the Arena and Romeo and Juliet, is a mecca for tourists. A visit to its most important monuments must include a stop at the Church of San Zeno Maggiore, one of Italy's masterpieces of Romanesque architecture, dedicated to the city's first bishop.

In the Middle Ages, the abbey of San Zeno reaped great benefits from the feudal system. It owned the pastures and the right to the products coming from Lessinia, an area enclosed by Val d'Adige, Valle dei Ronchi, Valle di Chiampo and the plains leading south. Perhaps due to its excellent climate, which combines the sub-Mediterranean, with an abundance of vineyards and olive groves, and the typical climate of the Alpine pastures, there have been shepherd communities here since ancient times (a colony of Bavarians was recorded here in the 13th century). Their activities included the production of a delicious cheese made from cows' milk.

Until recent times, this cheese was called simply *Monte Vernengo* or *Grasso Monte*, and it was a favorite in the markets of Brescia and Bergamo (contrarily, Verona was the distribution center for butter). The name Monte Veronese dates back to the beginning of the century and denotes a high quality product made from milk that comes from south-facing pastures which permit grazing for longer than usual, making it particularly fine.

Two milkings are used and coagulated together, after which the curd is matured. Trade regulations provide for the production of two types of cheese: a table cheese, which is aged for at least three months, and what is known as *d'allevo* cheese, for which partially skimmed milk is used and which is aged for no less than six months.

The cylindrical cheeses are about 10 cm in diameter, about 8 cm high, weigh about 8 kilos and have a fat content of about 34%.

The rind is very thin and elastic. The cheese ranges from white to a straw yellow, and is dotted with eyes, while the taste is pleasantly harmonious, and stronger in the *d'allevo* type. Monte Veronese is an excellent table cheese and a classic topping for polenta. When it is matured, it can also be grated.

PARMIGIANO REGGIANO

"In Berlinzone, in a locality called Bengodi, there was a mountain all made of grated parmesan," wrote Boccaccio in his *Decameron*, giving this cheese a place in the paradise of gastronomic joys. And there is truly no other cheese that can boast of such an ancient and glorious lineage as Parmigiano Reggiano. The cities of Parma and Reggio presented it to their royal guests; Pope Paul V preferred it to any other food, also using it as a cure for his bronchial ailments; the Republic of Venice sent it as an incomparable delicacy to the Pasha of Constantinople; while the aged Molière, aware that Parmigiano Reggiano was both strengthening and easily digested, included it as a main ingredient in his diet.

The origin of this cheese dates

Not just grated: Parmigiano Reggiano is also a great table cheese.

Processing of the milk in huge copper vats: the first phase in making Parmigiano Reggiano.

50

*The bitterness
of the rocket,
the sweetness of
the shrimps
and the
tanginess of the
Parmigiano
Reggiano
complement
each other in
this dish.*

Recipe

***SHRIMPS WITH ROCKET
AND PARMIGIANO REGGIANO***

Ingredients:
1 kg / 2 pounds shrimps
1 bunch rocket
*250 g / ½ pound Parmigiano
Reggiano*
2 lemons
*100 g / 3 ½ ounces extra-virgin
olive oil from west Liguria*
salt and pepper to taste

*Steam and peel the shrimps. Wash
the rocket and season with a
vinaigrette of oil, lemon, salt and
pepper, and arrange with the
shrimps. Finish by covering with
grated Parmigiano Reggiano.*

back to the Benedictine monks
of the 12th century who
experimented with a new
method of cheese-making
where the milk was heated
twice, first at a low temperature
and then at a high temperature,
breaking the curd into tiny
pieces with a hawthorn branch
(*biancospino* in Italian, from
which the word *spino*, the
utensil still used today to make

the cheese, is derived). The
result was so gratifying that the
monks started special
production. As scholar Mario
Iotti notes in his monumental
volume *Storia del Formaggio di
grana Parmigiano Reggiano*,
the areas of production
coincided with the dairy farms
of the Abbey of San Giovanni
Evangelista, Parma, in "the
territory of Villa Cella-Campegine

(west of Reggio) or in that part of the area west of the Taro River" near the present Castelguelfo in the province of Parma.

Numerous small milk production centers have since sprung up throughout the entire area. The structure of these *caselli* remained unchanged throughout the 19th century. Practically speaking, they were square structures, with brick pillars supporting a wooden roof, divided into three rooms: the first where the milk was processed, the salting room and the maturing cellar (the *casera*). Today, along with its age-old tradition, the selling point of Parmigiano Reggiano lies in the high standards of quality imposed by rigorous trade regulations. The milk comes from impeccably healthy animals fed with meadow fodder. The evening milking is left to rest in special tanks, allowing the fat (later used to make a tasty butter) to float naturally to the top, and then mixed with the whole milk from the morning milking. The entire mixture is poured into huge copper heating vats and allowed to coagulate. The curd is broken up into tiny grains using a *spino*, a large, round, whisk-like object with teeth on a long pole. It is then cooked at a temperature of 55°C, allowed to drain and left to rest in the molds for two or three days. Salting is carried out in brine for 20 to 24 days. At this point the cheese is ready for maturing, which lasts for at least a year.

The end result is unrivalled, thanks to a unique set of human, technical and climatic factors. It is no accident that Italian immigrants to Argentina who attempted to make a "South American parmesan cheese" with similar methods failed. Processing requires a heavy outlay in terms of labor and equipment and every single cheese is subject to strict controls before being put on the market with the consortium label. The production zone includes the provinces of Parma, Reggio and Modena and the areas west of the Reno River in the province of Bologna and east of the Po in the province of Mantua.

The cheeses are cylindrical, range from 35 to 45 cm in diameter, 18 to 24 cm each side or *scalzo* and weigh not less than 24 kilos. The slightly oily, golden yellow rind is over half a centimeter thick and the cheese is crumbly and grainy with a color ranging from white to ivory to a more intense yellow. Gastronomically, Parmigiano Reggiano has an elegant aroma and a distinct, savory, harmonious taste which is rich in complex variations, from the milder tones found in the younger "table" varieties to a stronger taste in the mature cheese. Its nutritional value is renowned (it is no accident that astronaut Cheli obtained NASA's

Breaking up the curd with a "spino".

- *Spumante Metodo Classico - G. Ferrari*

- *Tignanello - Marchesi Antinori*
- *Barbaresco Sorì Tildin - A. Gaja*
- *Amarone della Valpolicella*

permission to take it on board the *Columbus*). Moreover, since its grains consist of none other than tyrosine crystals, an amino acid linked to the digestive process, Parmigiano Reggiano is the most digestible cheese known. As with Gruyère in French cuisine, it is a basic ingredient in many of the great recipes of classic Italian cooking (the vast repertoire of soups, pastas and risottos, for instance) while it is also common as a topping (in fried foods and gratins) and as a condiment.

The special consortium label is branded onto the rind of every cheese.

FORMAGGIO DI FOSSA DI SOGLIANO AL RUBICONE E TALAMELLO

Romagna is by definition the land of good food. It is no accident that Pellegrino Artusi, the 19th-century scholar who first cataloged Italian cuisine, was born nearby, in the shadow of the imposing fortress of Forlimpopoli. And the tradition of Formaggio di Fossa lives right here, at Sogliano on the Rubicon, in the province of Forlì, and in the town of Talamello, only about ten kilometers away but part of the province of Pesaro. The origin of this cheese is not known with any certainty, but it

Artusi considered Passatelli in broth to be Romagna's most characteristic soup.

probably dates back to the raids of the Middle Ages and the need to hide the cheese from the greed of the passing soldiers. The Formaggio di Fossa cheeses – made from mixed milk or exclusively from ewes' milk – are dropped into the caves scattered throughout the area towards mid-August. The caves are carved out of sulphurous tufa rock and are shaped something like a flask, three or four meters deep, two meters wide at the bottom and a little less than a meter wide at the opening. Before the cheeses are deposited, they are placed into hermetically sealed white canvas bags and the caves are disinfected with a bonfire and covered with straw and wooden poles.

The bags are deposited in layers, one on top of another, and more wooden poles and sand are placed on top of the pile. Maturing lasts until November 25, the festival of Saint Catherine. Then the cheeses are pulled out and their unmistakable aroma wafts over the town – the poet Tonino Guerra described Formaggio di Fossa from Talamello as amber – and for many the cheese seems to evoke the depths of the earth.

Given the complexity of its taste and aroma, Formaggio di Fossa deserves to be enjoyed meditatively. The more Mature varieties can also be grated (in which case they are a valid alternative to Parmesan in the typical *Passatelli* in broth).

Suggested wines

- CHARDONNAY - GRAVNER
- ALBANA DI ROMAGNA PASSITA SCACCO MATTO - ZERBINA

- VINO NOBILE DI MONTEPULCIANO

Ugly to look at, Formaggio di Fossa has a delicious center.

PECORINO TOSCANO

Between 1459 and 1462, with the help of architect Bernardo Rossellino, Pio II Piccolomini, the "cultural pope", built the city of Pienza on the peak of a hill overlooking the Val d'Orcia, modelled on the humanist tradition with its love of perfection. A visit to the piazza

Recipe

COUNTRY-STYLE CAKE WITH PECORINO AND WALNUTS

Ingredients:
250 g / ½ pound young Pecorino Toscano
150 g / 5 ounces very fresh ewes' milk ricotta
300 g / 10 ounces flour
300 g / 10 ounces crushed walnut kernels
300 g / 10 ounces brisée pastry
15 eggs
200 g / 7 ounces sugar
150 g / 5 ounces potato starch
60 g / 2 ounces strawberry-tree honey

Take three eggs and whisk them together with the sugar and honey until they are light and frothy. Carefully blend in the sifted Pecorino, the Ricotta, the potato starch, the flour and the walnuts, adding 12 egg whites beaten until quite stiff. Pour the mixture into a cake mold lined with the pastry, spread evenly and bake in a 160°C oven for at least 45 minutes. Before serving, cover with an even layer of icing sugar and whole pieces of walnut.

Pecorino and walnut cake is a recipe that has almost disappeared from the Siena countryside.

Suggested wines

- BATARD - TENUTA QUERCIABELLA

- CHIANTI CLASSICO
- VINO NOBILE DI MONTEPULCIANO
- MASSETO - TENUTA DELL'ORNELLAIA

which opens up in the middle of this town is a must. The historical Communal Palace, the cathedral and the Palazzo Piccolomini dominate the square. But this pope, who so loved beauty, was also very fond of the pleasures of life. Indeed, one of his favorite foods was Pecorino from Siena, which he obtained from the best producers, branding his insignia into the rind.

Pecorino, known simply as *cacio*, meaning cheese par excellence, is widely produced in Tuscany, from Garfagnana to Chianti, Maremma to Casentino. The flavor and different "trade secrets" for its production vary from one location to another (sometimes vegetable rennet, like artichoke hearts, is used instead of the currently popular calf's rennet).

Tuscan Pecorino is also produced in Umbria, in parts of the province of Perugia near Lake Trasimeno and in upper Lazio, near the Lake of Bolsena. Production follows strict rules. Once the milk (ewes' milk only) has been coagulated, the curd is broken into pieces as large as hazelnuts (for soft Pecorino) or the size of corn kernels (for the hard variety). The batch is then placed in shallow molds cylindrical forms (they weigh between 1 and 3 kilos), and the whey is drained off by hand or with a fermenter in special rooms. The cheese is immediately matured in cool chambers with very high humidity: no less than three weeks for soft cheese and at least four months for hard cheese.

The color varies from white, with minute eyes and an elastic, straw-yellow rind, to a deeper yellow in the riper varieties. It has an intense aroma and a distinct, fragrant taste.

Pecorino has various uses: it is excellent with wine, as it was once served in Tuscan taverns, and it is also good for grating. It is also delicious with salads, with walnuts, pears or even – for the less mature variety – with honey. The idea of combining this cheese with something sweet is actually quite ancient. At the Carnival of Siena in 1719, the allegory of jealousy was portrayed as the blend of jam and *cacio*.

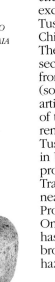

In Tuscany, Pecorino is often simply called "cacio", meaning cheese.

CASCIOTTA DI URBINO

The term *casciotta* is simply the local name for *caciotta* in Urbino and Pesaro where this cheese of noble and ancient origin is produced. The dukes of Urbino supervised production so that, for instance, Ubaldo II's Constitution of 1545 highly recommended that this cheese be made with the milk of local sheep rather than those of Maremma, the latter being more profitable in terms of quantity but not in terms of quality. An intelligent system of revenues and excise duties facilitated export to Rome and the Papal States, where many families from Urbino were settled. Francesco Amatori, an attendant from Castel Durante (one of the best areas of production), helped Michelangelo to purchase a series of farms in the zone from which he received regular shipments of this cheese of which he was so fond.

The main characteristic of Casciotta is its size. The cheeses weigh between 800 and 1200 grams and are ideal for selling whole. High quality ewes' milk is used, with the possible addition of 25% cows' milk. After coagulation, the batch is placed in special molds (made of ceramic in the Urbino area, with a hole in the bottom for the whey to drain out, while they are made of maple or beech wood in the territory around Pesaro), hand pressed and matured for between 15 and 30 days. The rind is thin and elastic and the cheese is firm and crumbly. It is a lovely whitish color with a delicate, pleasantly milky taste and a fat content of 45%. Casciotta is an excellent table cheese and it also goes well with fruit jam or aromatic honey.

Suggested wines

• *VERDICCHIO DI MATELICA*

• *DOLCETTO DI OVADA*
• *TEROLDEGO ROTALIANO*
• *ROSSO CONERO*

PECORINO ROMANO

Recipe

BUCATINI ALLA "GRICIA"

Ingredients:
350 g / 12 ounces Bucatini
10 cl / ¼ cup extra-virgin olive oil
from Sabina
1 chili pepper
2 cloves of garlic
200 g / 7 ounces salted bacon
200 g / 7 ounces grated Pecorino
black pepper and salt

Sauté the garlic until golden and add the bacon cut into thin strips along with the red pepper. Boil the Bucatini until it is al dente and add the drained pasta to the pan, ensuring that the cooking times coincide so that the bacon is soft but not yet crisp. Mix with some of the grated Pecorino while still in the pan. Then remove the pasta from the heat and generously sprinkle with the black pepper, coarsely ground in a mortar (hence the term "gricia", gray), grated Pecorino and a little olive oil.

The ancient Roman poet Virgil mentions a sauce called *moretum*, made with four cloves of garlic, parsley, rue, coriander, salt, fresh *cacio* (cheese), oil and a drop of strong vinegar, to be eaten as a merry accompaniment to a hot salted *focaccetta* (similar to pizza). In his treatise *De Re Rustica*, the 1st century scholar Columella describes ways of making cheese which might still be used today. Cheese-making is one of the oldest traditions of the Lazio countryside, and even though Pecorino has conquered markets all over the world (especially in the United States, which consumes 60% of the entire production), it is an exemplar of a cheese with an ancient heart. A crucial date in its evolution was 1884, when a papal ordinance forbid the *pizzicaroli* - the city shops where the *caciaro*, the cheese-makers, brought the cheeses for salting and maturing – to process the cheese within the city walls.

Thus cheese-making was moved to the countryside. The growing need for high quality milk caused the producers to turn to Sardinia, a country where shepherding was highly developed. Today, in fact, Pecorino is produced in Lazio, Sardinia and lower Maremma near Grosseto. Only the milk of sheep raised in natural pastures is used. It is collected from October to July, filtered and then milk enzymes are added (the *scotta-innesto*, or graft), which aids fermentation. Lamb rennet is used to coagulate the milk and the curd is then broken up into pieces the size of grains of rice. Traditionally, at this point, *frugatura* took place: a reed was inserted in the curd to let the whey run out. Today large drainage tanks are used and the cheese is then divided among the wooden cheese molds (the *fascere*). After pressing and fermenting, the Pecorino is dry salted and is matured for between five and eight months (for table and grating cheese respectively). The cylindrical cheeses are about 30 cm in diameter and weigh about thirty kilos. The cheese is pale straw yellow white and very firm, with a fat content of no less than 36%. As it ages, it darkens and tends to become crumbly. It has an intense aroma and a pleasant savory-strong taste.

An excellent grating cheese, it is traditionally eaten in the springtime in the Roman countryside with fresh broad beans, a pretext for boisterous drinking bouts with Frascati wine.

Bucatini alla gricia: the mixture of pepper and Pecorino makes the pasta gray.

MOZZARELLA DI BUFALA CAMPANA

There is disagreement as to how buffalo reached Italy. Some experts, basing their opinions on vague, ancient Roman documents, believe they are native, others believe they were brought by the Norman kings in Sicily and still others attribute their arrival to Agilulf and his Lombards. What is certain is that these semi-wild animals were used because of their strength and their huge hoofs to plow the marshy terrain where they thrive: buffalo have no sweat glands and need water to cool themselves down. This is also why raising these animals was once associated with stories of terrible suffering in inhospitable, malaria infested terrain (the testimony of Rocco Scotellaro is very evocative: he recalls that each animal had a name which was part of a sort of melancholy chant and was used to call it at milking-time). Real Mozzarella is all the rage today but it was also highly valued in the past, although consumption was limited to the areas of production since it was so difficult to preserve (the cheese was once wrapped in myrtle leaves and taken to the market in wooden baskets). Going back in time, we find that the medieval monks of Capua never refused bread and *mozza* to pilgrims, but also that, at the beginning of the 1600s, Mozzarella was traded for gold and wheat in the markets of Naples and Capua.

Today, the heart of the production area is found in the provinces of Caserta and Salerno, large areas of Campania, and some towns in the provinces of Frosinone, Latina and Rome.

The cheese is made with creamy buffalo milk, which has been pasteurized and acidified with the *cizza*, part of the whey from the day before. The milk is coagulated with calf rennet and the curd is worked to obtain grains the size of walnuts. The batch is cut into pieces and left to rest on slanted tables so that it can drain well.

The next phase is the very important "spinning" phase. The cheese is cut into thin slices and melted in a huge wooden vat to which boiling water is added. This melted mixture, shiny and elastic, is spun and then shaped (this was once done manually, and the cheese was *mozzata*, or cut

The taste of genuine breaded, fried Buffalo Mozzarella is incomparable.

off, with the thumbs and index fingers, the origin, apparently, of the name *mozzarella*) and dipped into cold water. Salting is carried out immediately afterwards in a procedure lasting more or less eight hours.
Mozzarella in its various forms (*treccia, ovoline, bocconcini, ciliegine*) is fresh, moist and elastic. It is a porcelain white cheese without eyes, and it has a very thin rind and a fat content of no less than 52%.

When cut, fragrant milk enzymes ooze out. Mozzarella has a full, slightly acid taste with a delicate hint of musk from the marshy areas where the buffalo graze.
There are numerous dishes made with Mozzarella, from the classic *caprese*, a salad made of Mozzarella, sliced tomatoes and fresh sweet basil leaves, to *pizza margherita* (the classic pizza with tomato sauce and Mozzarella) and *melanzane alla parmigiana*.

Suggested wines

- *Biancolella Tenuta Frassitelli*
  - D'Ambra Vini d'Ischia
- *Riviera Ligure di Ponente Pigato*
- *Franciacorta Gran Cuvée Pas Operé*
  - Bellavista

CANESTRATO PUGLIESE

• *Muffato - Castello della Sala*

• *Salice Salentino Rosso*
• *Sangiovese di Romagna*
• *Montepulciano d'Abruzzo - Valentini*

The region of Puglia is a recent discovery for tourists, and their enthusiasm is more than justified. There are countless things to see, but in few places is there such an impressive balance between the natural charm of the landscape and the beauty of the works of art as in the province of Foggia. Here one can admire the famous Gargano promontory and Tavoliere, not to mention Vieste and Manfredonia. And it is in the province of Foggia, as well as in some towns around Bari, that the famous Canestrato is produced. Canestrato is a savory, austere cheese with strong links to the ancient traditions of shepherding. With the practice of transhumance (the movement of the flocks towards the Abruzzo pastures during the good weather), this cheese spread throughout much of southern Italy. Gone is the bailiff who was the land-owner's right-hand man, the *caciaro*, the cheese-maker who took care of the milk and cheese, the herdsman who sheared the sheep, the *luparo* who protected the flocks from the wolves, the *toparo* who cleaned the stables, with all the band of shepherds who lent a hand (including the *fiscellari*, the basket weavers, who fashioned baskets and hampers out of Puglia's soft rushes, which are excellent for preserving cheese). But the method for producing Canestrato is still the same as in the past. Only the milk of sheep that graze in the wild and are milked no more than twice a day to obtain a richer product is used.

After coagulation with animal rennet, the cheeses are placed in baskets (hence the typical rough rind). The cheese is pressed regularly for about two months to eliminate excess moisture and salted either in brine or using the traditional methods of dry salting where coarse salt is spread over the rind. Canestrato can be sold after about ten months. The rind is brownish and the color of the cheese is various shades of straw yellow, depending on how long it was aged, with a firm or crumbly consistency. The fat content is about 38% and the taste is pleasantly strong and long-lasting.

CACIOCAVALLO SILANO

Calabria has earned a great reputation among tourists for its beaches with their clear, aquamarine water. But, despite the difficulties of the narrow, winding roads, it is worth a visit to the region's Apennine interior, where nature is still beautiful and uncontaminated. Art lovers can discover beautiful churches at Serra San Bruno or San Giovanni in Fiore, or important vestiges of Roman civilization at Marano (also known for its excellent preserves).

This stringy cheese, typical of the southern region (the area of production comprises Calabria, Molise, Basilicata and some areas of Campania and Puglia), unquestionably dates back to

Once, Caciocavallo Silano was aged in pairs on a rod, resembling "cacio a cavallo", cheese on horseback.

Recipe

STUFFED EGGPLANT

Ingredients:
6 eggplants
750 g / 1 ½ pounds tomatoes
300 g / 7 ounces young
Caciocavallo Silano
6 salted anchovies
4 cloves garlic
2 onions
capers, sweet basil, oil, salt and
pepper to taste

Sauté the diced onion in the oil and cook the chopped tomatoes (previously dipped briefly in boiling water to eliminate the liquid) for half an hour, adding salt and pepper. Stir in the basil, capers, garlic, the cleaned and rinsed anchovies and the finely diced Caciocavallo and cook for another few minutes. Take out the central part of the eggplant with the seeds, cover with oil, salt and pepper and bake in the oven for ten minutes at 200°C. Then fill the eggplant with the tomato-cheese mixture and return to the oven for another 15-20 minutes.

A fairly young Caciocavallo is needed to make the delicious stuffed eggplant in the recipe.

very ancient times. The name apparently derives from the custom of setting a pair of the cheeses to age on a rod so they seem to be riding horseback (*cacio a cavallo*, cheese on horseback).

There is also no doubt that other similar types of cheese such as the Turkish *qasqaval*, the Bosnian *kackvalj* and many other cheeses with similar names found throughout the Balkans, Bulgaria and Russia are derived from the Italian cheese.

Caciocavallo is made with cows' milk coagulated with calf or kid rennet paste. The curd is broken up into pieces the size of cherries and left to ripen until the consistency is stringy and rubbery (cheese-makers test the cheese by throwing some bits into boiling water).

The thick strand of cheese is shaped by hand into the classic oval or truncated cone-shaped forms, ensuring that the surface remains smooth. The top of the cheese is closed by dipping it into boiling water (one option, depending on the local custom, is to mold a roundish head on the top). Then the cheese is salted in brine. The maturing process can last from two weeks to several months.

The rind of Caciocavallo Silano is smooth, thin and straw yellow while the inside is between white and pale yellow. The young cheese has a harmonious, pleasantly aromatic taste which tends to become stronger as it ages. It is an excellent table cheese and, since it melts well, is ideal for a large number of recipes. The fat content is 38%.

RAGUSANO

One of the loveliest monuments in Ragusa, Sicily, is the beautiful San Giorgio Church which stands at the pinnacle of a steep flight of steps, with its precious baroque façade. Its opulent appearance is in sharp contrast to the simple, rustic image of Caciocavallo Ragusano, one of the great products of a cheese-making tradition which has always been penalized by the large landowners. The cheese's name in local dialect, *scaluni*, meaning steps, refers to the rectangular forms almost half a meter long and 15 cm high, weighing around 15 kilos; steps towards excellence, whose milk comes from the local breed, called *modicana*, found in a territory covering the provinces of Ragusa and Siracusa.

The milk is coagulated with lamb or kid rennet paste and

Recipe

RAGUSANO WITH OREGANO

Ingredients:
500 g / 1 pound Caciocavallo Ragusano
2 cloves garlic
extra-virgin olive oil, red wine vinegar and oregano to taste

Sauté the garlic in oil in a large, earthenware pan and lay slices of the cheese on top, taking care not to overlap. Brown the mixture, moistening with red wine vinegar and serve generously sprinkled with oregano.

Sicilian oregano and a dash of red wine vinegar transform this delicious recipe based on melted Ragusano.

Suggested wines

• ARCHETIPI COLLIO SAUVIGNON - PUIATTI

• DUCA ENRICO - DUCA DI SALAPARUTA
VINI CORVO
• CABERNET SAUVIGNON -
TASCA D'ALMERITA REGALEALI
• TAURASI

the curd is broken up into tiny grains, adding water heated to 80°C. The cheeses are then worked into the characteristic rectangular form. The cheeses are salted in brine and matured by hanging in pairs on special ropes so that they can breathe. The cheeses are brushed with oil and vinegar on the outside to keep undesirable insects, larvae or mildew away. The cheeses are ready for sale after a period of four months (for table cheese) and six months (for grating cheese).

The hard cheese, a lovely white color which becomes straw colored with aging, easily splits with time. It has an intense aroma and a taste ranging from mild and aromatic to strong. It is an excellent table and grating cheese and, because it is stringy, is ideal for cooking.

The unusual shape of this cheese has earned it the name "scaluni", meaning steps in local dialect.

PECORINO SICILIANO

The term Pecorino Siciliano refers exclusively to an age-old cheese produced with ewes' milk, found all over Sicily (a legend even attributes it to the cyclopes shepherd Polyphemus extolled by Homer in the *Odyssey*). Because Pecorino, the very epitome of cheese, is so common throughout the island, it takes on different names according to its appearance or production technique. So we have *canestrato*, basket cheese, bearing the imprint of the rushes in which it is cured; *maiorchino* for the type that matures during March; the entire *primo sale,* first salting range and the *pepato*, peppered cheese for a type not on the official list which, as with Arab cheeses, is made by mixing the curd with black peppercorns. Ancient rituals are rigorously followed when making this cheese. The coagulated milk is broken into tiny pieces and water heated to 75 °C is added. The batch is extracted in rush baskets before being placed in the cylindrical molds. Pressing takes place by hand and the cheese is dry salted up to three times over a two month period. The cheeses, weighing between 4 and 12 kilos, have an amber rind while the interior is straw white and hard. The aroma is quite intense and the taste rich and strong.

Suggested wines

- *Chardonnay -*
Tasca d'Almerita Regaleali
- *Marsala Vergine Terre Arse -*
Vinicola Italiana Florio

- *Rosso Conero*
- *Alto Adige Cabernet Lowengang -*
Lageder

PECORINO SARDO

Recipe

"QUATTA" SOUP

Ingredients:
2 l / 8 cups lamb and vegetable stock
1 loaf home-made type bread
500 g / 1 pound mild Pecorino Sardo
salt and black pepper to taste

In a baking dish, lay alternating layers of bread and the Pecorino cut into thin strips, ending with the cheese. Cover with the hot stock and bake in a pre-heated oven at 200°C for at least 30 minutes.

Suggested wines

- *CAPICHERA - TENUTA CAPICHERA*
- *GAVI DI GAVI*

- *MARCHESE DI VILLAMARINA - SELLA & MOSCA*
- *SAN GIORGIO - CANTINE LUNGAROTTI*

Tourists identify Sardinia with its beaches, its limpid sea, its rocky inlets and the luxurious Emerald Coast. But to encounter the real spirit of the Sardinia of olden times, one must leave the coast and travel inland. The wild beauty of the landscape stretches from scrubland to the mountains. At Barùmini, you can visit the *nuraghi* of Su Nuraxi, dating back to megalithic civilization (13th century B.C.), an impressive fortress surrounded by a Bronze Age village from the 8th century B.C. It is as well to keep these images in mind when thinking about what is today called Pecorino Sardo but which used to be called simply *semicotto* (half-cooked), a product which has become extremely popular since the World War II. Trade regulations allow production throughout Sardinia and recognize two types, "mild" and "mature". Both are made with coagulated whole ewes' milk; the curd of the mild variety is broken up into pieces the size of walnuts and the mature variety is reduced to bits as small as rice grains.

The cheese is then cured for between 20 and 60 days for the mild type, and from two to twelve months for the mature variety.

Mild Pecorino has a smooth, pale rind. It is a soft white cheese with a harmonious, mild, slightly aromatic taste. The mature variety has a harder, darker rind and the cheese is straw-yellow, tending to become crumbly and decidedly strong with age. The fat content is around 40%.

FIORE SARDO

Suggested wines

- *TERRE BIANCHE - SELLA & MOSCA*
- *CINQUETERRE SCIACCHETRÀ*
- *ALBANA DI ROMAGNA PASSITA SCACCO*
- *MATTO - ZERBINA*

- *TANCA FARRÀ - SELLA & MOSCA*

The appeal of Fiore Sardo lies in the way it is produced, based on the ancient manual method used by shepherds. Ewes' milk from the Sardinian breed which apparently evolved from the ancient moufflon (still to be found on the island) is used exclusively, and is still worked by the shepherds' families. They once produced it in their circular huts whose stone walls supported a roof of branches or *pinnette*, from which the smoke from the central fire could escape. Today, the milk is no longer heated with red-hot stones in a wooden vat. Instead it is coagulated with lamb or kid's rennet, and the curd placed in the characteristic truncated cone-shaped molds, dipped in boiling water (making for a thicker rind), salted and left to rest on the *cannitto*, a sort of ledge made of reeds set above the fireplace, so becoming slightly smoked. After that, the cheese is cured in a sort of attic for some time, and then moved to damp, cool, underground areas where the women rub the rind with oil or sheep fat to keep it from drying out. Maturing takes from three to six months and the cheeses weighing between a kilo and a half and 4 kilos, have a deep yellow rind while the interior is ivory or straw colored with a fat content of about 40%. The cheese has a decisive taste, aromatic and medium-strong. In the past, it was a basic food in the daily diet and the grating cheese was exported. It was especially appreciated in Genoa where it was an essential ingredient of the classic *pesto*.